The Economic and Environmental Sustainability of Dual Sourcing

Forschungsergebnisse der Wirtschaftsuniversität Wien

Band 54

Frankfurt am Main · Berlin · Bern · Bruxelles · New York · Oxford · Wien

HEIDRUN ROSIČ

The Economic and Environmental Sustainability of Dual Sourcing

PETER LANG
Internationaler Verlag der Wissenschaften

Bibliographic Information published by the Deutsche Nationalbibliothek
The Deutsche Nationalbibliothek lists this publication in the Deutsche Nationalbibliografie; detailed bibliographic data is available in the internet at http://dnb.d-nb.de.

Sponsored by the Vienna University
of Economics and Business.

Cover design:
Atelier Platen according to a design of
Werner Weißhappl.

University logo of the Vienna University
of Economics and Business:
Printed with kind permission of the University.

ISSN 1613-3056
ISBN 978-3-631-62272-8
© Peter Lang GmbH
Internationaler Verlag der Wissenschaften
Frankfurt am Main 2012
All rights reserved.

www.peterlang.de

Für meine Familie

Contents

List of Figures

List of Tables

Chapter 1

Introduction

1.1 Motivation

Supply chains consist of all processes which are needed in order to supply customers with the required products. These are, for instance, sourcing, production, transport or warehousing processes. Traditionally supply chain management decisions are based on the economic performance of the parties involved which can be expressed by (non-)financial measures, like profit or total landed costs and customer service (see, for instance, Chopra and Meindl, 2010, van Mieghem, 2008). Based on the economic performance measures, different supply chain strategies, like outsourcing and offshoring, which is the relocation of production activities to low-cost countries, or centralization of production or warehousing facilities have turned out to be advantageous in certain industries. These strategies lead to a reduction of procurement or production costs in the case of outsourcing and offshoring. By centralizing production facilities economies of scale can be exploited; in the case of centralization of warehousing facilities inventory costs can be reduced due to risk pooling effects (see, e.g., Anupindi et al., 2006, Chopra and Meindl, 2010). But as a negative side-effect supply chains become longer and/or more complex (Tang, 2006). Due to the increased length of supply chains, in general, more transport activities are necessary leading to an increase of the respective costs. Furthermore, even though some of the transport can be shifted to more environmentally friendly modes, such as sea transport, in general, the strategies go hand in hand with higher carbon emissions from transport.

In recent years, besides economic performance measures other criteria, like flexibility, quality or the environment, have become important as well (Ferreira and Prokopets, 2009). Environmental issues, especially carbon emissions related to the activities of companies, rank high on the political agenda because they are considered to be a major cause of the greenhouse gas effect (IPCC, 2007). Based on this, regulations concerning carbon emissions of companies' activities have already been introduced. One example is the EU emission trading scheme (ETS) which restricts the carbon emissions of energy-intensive industries within the European Union (European Community, 2005). Beside these industries, which account for approximately half of the carbon emissions, transport is the second largest polluter (Eurostat, 2009). Therefore, stricter regulations with respect to carbon emissions of transport are expected to be introduced. For instance, based on an EU directive agreed in 2008 (European

Community, 2008) aviation will be included in the EU ETS by 2012. Alternatively, a transport carbon emission tax or charge may be introduced to make companies pay some part of the external costs of transport.

Beside the pressure of new regulations Walker et al. (2008) point out other drivers for "green" supply chain management, such as customer awareness with respect to the environmental impact of products, the personal commitment of managers or internal cost reduction initiatives. Due to these internal and external drivers companies start to consider the environment in their decision-making. It can be concluded that mainly stricter regulations and increasing customer awareness encourage companies to reconsider their strategies by incorporating the environmental dimension in supply chain management decisions. Companies have to search for strategies that are at the same time cost-efficient, provide the required customer service and have a low negative impact on the environment. Furthermore, companies will have to deal with more stringent regulations concerning carbon emissions.

1.2 Purpose of the work

In addition to economic performance measures, like total landed costs or profit and customer service, a further dimension, i.e. the environment, should be included in supply chain management decisions. Based on economic performance measures strategies, like offshoring, outsourcing of production and centralization inventory locations, are pursued in various industries. Often a single offshore sourcing strategy is pursued in order to lower product unit costs whereby the increase of transport costs is often negligible compared to the reductions of procurement costs. Transport activities, however, have a negative impact on the environment, mainly due to the carbon emissions produced by the use of fossil fuels, and should therefore be reduced from the viewpoint of environmental sustainability. Furthermore, it is to be expected that stricter regulations will be imposed on the transport sector, like the introduction of a carbon emission tax or the implementation of a carbon emission trading scheme for the transport sector.

Some work has already been done with regards to considering environmental criteria in supply chain management decisions. But, to the best of our knowledge, not much work has been done with respect to including the environmental impact of transport into the sourcing and ordering decision. To fill a part of this research gap, we compare a single offshore sourcing strategy with a dual sourcing strategy relying on an offshore and an onshore supplier. For the modelling, we rely on the newsvendor framework. The offshore supplier is cheap but is far away from the market. It has a long lead time and is therefore slow and inflexible. The onshore supplier is close to the market and flexible. It can deliver on short notice but is expensive. Past work has already shown that this strategy can help companies to improve the performance with respect to expected profit and customer service (see, for instance, Warburton and Stratton, 2005, Cachon and Terwiesch, 2009).

In addition to the economic performance, we evaluate the dual sourcing strategy based on the environmental dimension, i.e. the carbon emissions from transport which are directly related to the quantity ordered from the offshore supplier. We also consider regulations concerning carbon emissions from transport in the model and evaluate the effect of these regulations on the decision-making of individual companies. In the first step, we analyse the effect of a strict limit (constraint) on carbon emissions from transport. In the second step, we consider a linear carbon emission tax on transport and in the third step, we assume that an emission trading system is valid which also includes the transport sector. We analyse how the optimal ordering decision is influenced by including these additional parameters. Furthermore, we have a closer look at the development of the profitability of the supply chain and at the differences with respect to order quantities and the related transport carbon emissions. A very interesting question in this respect is whether economic criteria and environmental criteria contradict each other. In other words, is there a trade-off between economic and environmental performance of supply chains? Or can a supply chain at the same time perform well on the three dimensions, i.e. expected profit, customer service and carbon emissions? We provide analytical and numerical results and perform sensitivity analyses. Based on the results, we derive implications for management and policy-making.

1.3 Structure of the work

In Section 2 we present, first, the basics of "traditional" supply chain management and give a brief overview of supply chain planning levels and the related decisions. Furthermore, we briefly deal with the drivers of supply chains and their impact on the economic performance of supply chains. Second, the focus is on defining the general term sustainability and its relation to supply chains. The focus of our work is on economic and environmental sustainability, excluding the social dimension, and therefore, we present conceptual works related to "green supply chain management". In addition to that, an overview of approaches of how to measure the carbon emissions resulting from supply chain activities is given. In this respect, the focus is on carbon emissions of transport and the respective calculation models and tools. This chapter ends with an overview of environmental regulations which have an impact on supply chains.

In Section 3 we provide an overview of works dealing with the integration of environmental aspects into supply chain decisions whereby we group the works according to the decision support which they provide. For our purpose, these are network design decisions, inventory (ordering) decisions, production mix and production planning decisions and transport mode choice and transport planning decisions. Basically, the environment can be integrated in decision-making by adding (a) constraint(s), by monetarisation of the environmental impact and including it in the cost or profit function or by using multi-objective programming approaches. We conclude this chapter with a summary of the existing work and point out the relations to our field of research.

Section 4 is the core of this work. First, we provide a short review of inventory management and the classical newsvendor model which is the cornerstone of our work. Second, we present an overview of sourcing strategies and deal in detail with dual sourcing in the newsvendor context. We, then, extend the economic evaluation of dual sourcing by also accounting for its environmental performance, i.e. carbon emissions from transport. For that purpose, we develop a transport-focused dual sourcing framework and we compare a single offshore sourcing strategy with a dual sourcing strategy relying on an offshore and an onshore supplier. This chapter comprises the basic single-period dual sourcing model based on the newsvendor framework and its extensions to account for environmental regulations with respect to transport carbon emissions. We provide analytical results as well as numerical analyses from which we derive implications for management and policy-making.

In Section 5 we discuss the general conclusions of our work and point out limitations as well as further research opportunities.

Chapter 2

Supply chains and their impact on the environment

2.1 Supply chain management

According to Chopra and Meindl (2010, p. 20) "a supply chain consists of all parties involved, directly or indirectly, in fulfilling a customer request. The supply chain includes not only the manufacturers and suppliers, but also transporters, warehouses, retailers, and even customers themselves." Supply chain management aims at designing, managing and coordinating material/product, information and financial flows to fulfil customer requirements at low costs and thereby increasing supply chain profitability. A definition by Simchi-Levi et al. (2008, p. 1) which is focused on the goods flow states that supply chain management comprises "[...] a set of approaches utilized to efficiently integrate suppliers, manufacturers, warehouses, and stores, so that merchandise is produced and distributed at the right quantities, to the right locations, and at the right time, in order to minimize systemwide costs while satisfying service level requirements."

Supply chain management decisions are traditionally evaluated based on the economic performance which can be expressed by financial and non-financial measures, such as total landed costs and customer service (van Mieghem, 2008). Customer service is directly related to product availability which can be measured in different ways. Two very important measures are the fill rate, which shows the fraction of demand which is satisfied immediately from inventory, and the cycle service level, which is the fraction of replenishment cycles which end without any stock-outs. The cycle service level, therefore, is the probability that all demand is met during a replenishment cycle. In general, there is a trade-off between efficiency and responsiveness – in other words between costs and customer service (Chopra and Meindl, 2010). Also for Nahmias (2009) the main trade-off in supply chain management is between cost and response time which is similar to the approach of Chopra and Meindl (2010). Obviously, the trade-off between efficiency and responsiveness has to be solved depending on the product characteristics and in accordance with the competitive strategy. According to Fisher (1997) a supply chain of a functional product has to be cost-efficient whereby a supply chain of an innovative product should be designed to be responsive.

According to Chopra and Meindl (2010) there are several key drivers of a supply chain which in combination determine the performance of a supply chain; they help to find the balance between efficiency and responsiveness that fits to the competitive strategy. The first three drivers (facilities, inventory and transportation) are denoted as functional drivers while the latter three (information, sourcing and pricing) are cross-functional drivers.

Facilities are the physical locations in a supply chain, which can be either production or storage sites. The decisions to be taken concern the role, the location, the capacity and the flexibility of a facility. By using only a limited number of facilities economies of scale can be achieved and benefits can result from risk pooling leading to lower total costs. However, the cost reduction, in general, comes at the expense of responsiveness due to an increased distance to downstream facilities and/or customers. A production facility can be either dedicated, flexible or a combination of the two. A flexible facility can produce a range of different products and thereby helps to increase the responsiveness in the supply chain but generally the company has to sacrifice efficiency for that. The opposite holds true for a dedicated facility which can only produce a limited number of products. In addition to that, the capacity of a facility has to be determined. Allowing for excess capacity increases flexibility and responsiveness but usually also increases the costs. Overall, it can be said that by increasing the number of facilities, facility and inventory costs increase but outbound transportation costs and response time can be reduced.

Inventory comprises all raw materials, work in process and (semi-)finished products in a supply chain. For the different types of inventory the adequate inventory policies have to be determined. Inventory generally results from a mismatch between demand and supply. This mismatch can be intentional to produce or order in large lots; or inventory can result from uncertainties on the demand side or in the production/procurement process. The level of inventory decisively determines the product availability which is directly related to responsiveness. However, the inventory held is also an important source of cost in a supply chain. So again, there is a trade-off between efficiency by lowering inventory and the related costs and responsiveness which can be achieved by holding high stock levels.

Transportation is the physical movement of goods between points in a supply chain. In order to realize the transport of goods, different modes (air, road, rail, inland waterways, sea or pipeline) and routes have to be combined either by the company itself when having its own fleet or by a logistics service provider. In addition to that, it has to be decided whether the transport is carried out directly or whether the goods go via intermediate points. By using a fast transport mode, such as air transport, the responsiveness in a supply chain can be undoubtedly increased but at the same time this results in high transport costs. In this respect, the relation to the other drivers must not be neglected as, for instance, using a fast transport mode generally results in lower inventories.

Information includes the data about facilities, inventory, transportation, costs, prices, customers, etc. in the supply chain. This driver affects every part of the supply chain and can help to increase efficiency and responsiveness simultaneously. In order to provide, analyse and share information within a supply chain various enabling technologies can be used, such as electronic data interchange for transmitting orders, radio frequency identification for tracking and tracing of goods, enterprise resource planning systems to administer data internally and supply chain management software or advanced planning software to provide decision support.

Sourcing comprises the choice of who will carry out an activity and is the process required to buy goods and services. It is linked to the make-or-buy decision of a company which determines the tasks to be carried out in-house and the tasks to be outsourced, i.e. the degree of vertical integration. If a task is outsourced, the company then has to decide how many suppliers to use and where the suppliers are located. These decisions together with the delivery conditions of a supplier have a huge impact on efficiency and responsiveness.

Pricing relates to decisions of how much to charge for the goods and service and how to use promotional and marketing tools. This driver can help to match supply and demand by using revenue management techniques.

The decisions which have to be taken in a supply chain fall into three phases which are supply chain design, supply chain planning and supply chain operations, whereby these decisions differ with respect to the frequency of decision-making and the time horizon upon which a decision has an impact. During the first phase the structure of a supply chain together with the capacities and location of facilities are determined and make-or-buy decisions are made. All these decisions have a long-term impact. In the second phase, the company decides which markets will be supplied from which locations, if subcontracting of manufacturing is done and the inventory policies are fixed. These decisions have a mid-term time horizon of a quarter to a year. On the operational level, short-term decisions are taken. For instance, detailed production plans or delivery schedules are fixed (Chopra and Meindl, 2010).

Fleischmann et al. (2008) follow a similar categorization based on Anthony (1965) for supply chain planning decisions. Planning refers to the preparation of a decision and decision-support by the identification of alternatives and se-

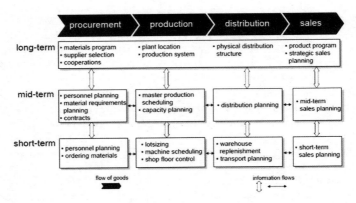

Figure 2.1: Supply chain planning matrix

Source: Fleischmann et al. (2008, p. 87)

lection of a good or the best solution (see, also, Domschke and Scholl, 2005). Planning can be supported by different operations research methods, such as linear programming, mixed integer programming, simulation, forecasting and similar. For an overview of operations research methods see, for instance, Hillier and Lieberman (2010). Fleischmann et al. (2008) distinguish between long-term (strategic) planning, mid-term planning and short-term planning. In addition to time horizon, the planning tasks for a supply chain can be categorized according to the supply chain processes, i.e. procurement, production, distribution and sales. By taking these two dimensions the supply chain planning matrix can be built which shows the different supply chain planning tasks. (see Figure 2.1). This matrix gives a good overview of the different decisions which have to be taken in order to design and operate a supply chain.

2.2 Sustainability of supply chains

According to the Brundtland Report (United Nations, 1987) sustainability is defined as "[...] development that meets the needs of the present without compromising the ability of future generations to meet their needs". In this respect, sustainability comprises three dimensions, namely economic, social and environmental sustainability. For several years now, researchers and practitioners in the field of operations management have been facing the challenge to integrate the issues of sustainability into the traditional way of thinking.

Based on the idea of sustainability approaches like the triple bottom line (3BL, TBL) (Elkington, 2004) which refers to reporting about the three Ps, i.e. people, profit and planet, have been developed (Kleindorfer et al., 2005). Studies have shown that the long-term success of a company can only be guaranteed if the concepts of sustainability are integrated in supply chain management. Companies which attempt to maximize the performance of all three dimensions outperform those only concentrating on economic performance or just achieving high social or environmental performance (Carter and Rogers, 2008).

Seuring and Müller (2008) present an extensive literature review and identify drivers and barriers for sustainable supply chain management which is defined as "[...] management of material, information and capital flows as well as cooperation among companies along the supply chain while taking goals from all three dimensions of sustainability, i.e., economic, environmental and social, into account which are derived from customer and stakeholder requirements." This means that sustainable supply chain management, in contrast to "traditional" supply chain management deals with a wider set of performance indicators and objectives. According to this survey the research is dominated by environmental issues; social aspects and the integration of all three dimensions in supply chain management are only rarely considered.

In this respect, Pagell and Zhaohui (2009) use case studies in order to develop a model of an integrated sustainable supply chain, whereby they consider both the environmental and the social aspects of sustainability. They, as well, point out that a sustainable supply chain "[...] performs well on both traditional measures of profit and loss as well as on an expanded conceptualization of performance that includes social and natural dimensions." For their study, they choose leaders in sustainable supply chain management from different industries and identify what distinguishes their business model from traditional supply chains. In more practical terms, in order to be sustainable a supply chain should seek to reduce greenhouse gases, the use of energy and water and avoid harmful substances in the design, manufacturing and distribution of products. In addition to that, sustainability goals should also include social responsibilities to employees, suppliers, customers and the community (Pedersen, 2009).

Also, Halldorsson et al. (2009) carry out a literature review about supply chain management and its relation to sustainability. In conclusion they point out that there are three approaches about how supply chain management can deal with the issue of sustainability distinguishing the integrated strategy, the alignment strategy and the replacement strategy. Following an integrated sustainability strategy means that current supply chain practices should be enhanced to consider environmental and social aspects. For that the notion of supply chain efficiency has to be broadened by also considering environmental and social performance measures. A balance between costs, service and environmental as well as social aspects has to be found. By using an alignment strategy which can be referred to the triple bottom line approach economic, social and environmental aspects are considered as complimentary. Equal weight is assigned to the three goals. For that purpose, the three dimensions have to be part of the company's mission statement. The replacement strategy assumes that supply chain management is in contradiction to sustainability assuming that, for instance, what is positive for the revenue of company automatically has a negative impact on the environment. So, in order to achieve sustainability a paradigm shift has to take place. This last strategy refers to more critical views on today's business actions to achieve sustainability. According to Ehrenfeld (2005) all actions are rather focused on "[...] reducing the unsustainability of a flawed economic development system [...]" than creating sustainability. According to that idea, in order to achieve sustainable development a fundamental change has to take place.

In particular, the impact of operations and supply chains on the environment has received increasing attention from governments, society and consumers in the recent past. Environmental criteria become more and more important for the decisions which have to be taken in the field of supply chain management. In our work we leave out the social dimension of the term sustainability and restrict it to the economic and environmental dimension.

2.3 Concepts of green supply chain management

A literature review about green supply chain management is provided by Srivastava (2007). According to him green supply chain management can be defined as "[...] integrating environmental thinking into supply-chain management, including product design, material sourcing and selection, manufacturing processes, delivery of the final product to the customer as well as end-of-life management of the product after its useful life." A topic which is very often covered in this respect is the recovery of used products, i.e. reverse logistics (see, e.g., Dyckhoff et al., 2004, Fleischmann et al., 1997), and the design and management of closed-loop supply chains (Flapper et al., 2005). In these works, it is assumed that the environmental performance is automatically improved when considering reverse flows in decision-making. According to Srivastava (2007) green supply chain management becomes more and more important because of various reasons. Firstly, the deterioration of the environment, such as the depletion of natural resources or higher levels of pollution, forces companies to consider the environment in their decisions. Secondly, regulations are imposed by national and international authorities with which companies have to comply. Thirdly, customers and the society put pressure on companies.

In this respect, Walker et al. (2008) identify drivers and barriers of green supply chain management practices based on a literature review. Then an explorative study is conducted with a small number of private and public sector organizations in order to verify the importance of the drivers and barriers. In accordance with Srivastava (2007) they differ between internal, i.e. organizational factors, and external drivers, i.e. regulation, customers, competition and society. Environmental supply chain management might be pushed by the personal motivation of managers or by cost reduction initiatives. But Walker et al. (2008) conclude from the conducted interviews that the external drivers are by far more important. Regulations are passed by national and international authorities and impose restrictions upon companies which can be proactive or reactive towards the legislative initiatives. Business customers put pressure on companies by, for instance, requiring certification. Consumers might change their shopping behaviour demanding "green" products to a greater extent. Competition can also be seen as a driver for environmental supply chain management as companies using environmentally friendly technology might gain a competitive advantage. Further, the companies leading in technology might be responsible for new industry standards and/or regulations. Finally, society and various stakeholder representatives, such as non-governmental organizations, encourage companies to act "green" in order to keep a certain reputation. Often, costs are considered as major barriers to environmental supply chain management by assuming that there is a clear trade-off economy and environment (Porter and van der Linde, 1995). But also lack of commitment from management and partners in the supply chain or regulations might be a barrier to the successful development of a green supply chain by hindering innovations.

Based on the idea that there is a trade-off between economy and ecology Huppes and Ishikawa (2005, 2007) have developed the concept of eco-efficiency which can be used for the environmental sustainability analysis of systems, such as supply chains. Eco-efficiency refers to "[...] a ratio between environmental impact and economic cost or value" (Huppes and Ishikawa, 2007). They refer back to a definition of eco-efficiency by Schmidheiny (1992) which was further developed by World Business Council on Sustainable Developement (2000) and Verfaillie and Bidwell (2000). Four types of eco-efficiency can be distinguished based on whether the focus is on value creation/cost reduction or environmental improvement. Environmental productivity and its inverse, environmental intensity of production, refer to the value creation aspect. Environmental productivity is defined as production or consumption value per unit of environmental impact; the environmental intensity is the environmental impact per unit of production or consumption value. In contrast to this, the environmental improvement cost, which is the cost per unit of environmental improvement, and its inverse, environmental cost-effectiveness, which shows the environmental improvement per unit of cost, are related to environmental improvement measures (Huppes and Ishikawa, 2007).

The work of Bloemhof-Ruwaard et al. (1995) is one of the first reviews about how operational research and environmental management (might) interact. They also identify future legal requirements and consumer pressure as the main drivers for integrating environmental issues into supply chain management. The central idea is that two interlinked chains exist, i.e. the supply chain and the environmental chain. On the one hand the supply chain impacts on ("harms") the environmental chain by producing waste, emissions and similar unwanted byproducts. On the other hand the environmental chain provides the resources for the supply chain to produce its output. Furthermore, changes in the environmental conditions have an influence on how a supply chain can operate and environmental regulations impose restrictions on supply chains. The same idea is reflected in the "inside-out/outside-in" relationship between companies and the environment which is suggested by Porter and Reinhardt (2007). Bloemhof-Ruwaard et al. (1995) point out different approaches of how the environment could be considered in company's decision-making process. The "end-of-pipe approach" relies on the idea to incorporate environmental issues as constraints into existing models. In contrast to this, preventive approaches require the development of new models and the use of different techniques. In addition to the integration of environmental issues into supply chain modelling they point out that operations research can support environmental policy-making. Daniel et al. (1997) extend the work of Bloemhof-Ruwaard et al. (1995) by carrying out a similar literature review.

Also Wu and Dunn (1995) underline that several environmental problems have been enforced or even created by economic activity. There is a two-sided relationship between supply chains and the environment; on the one hand, resources are used and converted into desired output products and on the other hand, undesired byproducts, such as waste and emissions, are the result of supply chain processes. Due to stricter regulations and higher customer awareness, environmentally responsible logistics systems have to be created which also have to meet cost and efficiency objectives. For that purpose, environmental objectives have to be added to the decision-making process on the different stages of the supply chain, such as raw material procurement, inbound and outbound logistics, the production process and the after-sales service. Several small examples on how to reduce the environmental impact are given, ranging from local sourcing, to the use of alternative transport modes and packaging reduction initiatives.

Angell and Klassen (1999) point out that much of the research in the area of environmental operations management "[...] has adopted a prescriptive tone, based on anecdotal evidence [...]" and they identify two perspectives, namely the external constraint perspective and the component perspective. While under the constraint perspective environmental performance requirements are considered as an externally imposed constraint, under the component perspective environmental issues are integrated into the operations strategy as a factor of its own. Based on a literature review and supported by a focus group, they develop a research agenda and identity research gaps. In their long list of research topics they point out several questions which refer to our work. These are, for instance:

- How do environmental issues impact supply chain management?
- How to integrate environmental issues into planning and decision-making and what are appropriate performance measures?
- How to include environmental variables in the objective function of traditional operations management and operations research?

Furthermore they underline the importance of applying environmental tools, such as life cycle analysis, in order to support environmentally sound decision-making.

Also, Inman (1999) point out that environmental considerations have to be included into production planning and control, inventory control and distribution and logistics. With respect to the first area he points out that existing models have to be adjusted in order to be applicable to disassembly processes. Concerning inventory planning he also focuses on the integration of the return flow into existing models (disassembly, reuse, recycling, repair, etc.). In the third area, the importance of integration of the two flows, i.e. forward and reverse, into logistics and transportation planning is underlined. This paper clearly shows that environmental supply chain management is often limited to the idea of considering return flows of supply chains. By doing that, it is assumed that the environmental performance of a supply chain is automatically enhanced. But this general statement has recently been doubted by, for instance, Quariguasi Frota Neto et al. (2009a).

The work of Klassen and Johnson (2004) highlights the past developments in green supply chain management and systematize green supply chain practices, i.e. environmental certification, pollution prevention, reverse logistics, life-cycle assessment and design for environment. They develop a framework for integrating supply chain orientation and environmental orientation. The supply chain orientation ranges from a transactional to a network orientation whereby the first refers to a short-term relation of the company with its partners in the supply chain and the latter denotes the establishment of long-term relations with key partners in order to exploit synergies. With respect to environmental orientation either a proactive or a reactive attitude of companies with respect to the environment can be witnessed. A proactive orientation means that a company anticipates new environmental issues and integrates these concerns in its decision-making. It is concluded that a transactional supply chain orientation limits the potential improvements from green supply chain management. Overall, the supply chain orientation has to be aligned with the environmental orientation in order to be successful in implementing a green supply chain practice. They conclude that for decades environmental issues have only been considered in the form of pollution control within a single firm, but over the past years the scope has been broadened first from a single firm to whole supply chains and second from control to actively prevent negative environmental impacts (Klassen and Johnson, 2004). Related to this, Tsoulfas and Pappis (2006) present environmental principles which have to be considered in the field of product design, packaging, collection and transportation, recycling and disposal, greening the internal and external business environment. The different approaches, such as packaging reduction, reduction of hazardous materials or increasing of recycling quotas, and their applicability are supported by case studies.

Bloemhof-Ruwaard and van Nunen (2005) present a framework for sustainable supply chain management and state that (environmental) sustainability can be attained by changing the network design and/or modes of transportation. They define sustainability according to the Brundtland report and in their concept all forward and reverse supply chain processes are included. All the processes have to be optimized considering ecological, economic and social objectives. They distinguish two major fields, namely closed-loop supply chains, comprising reverse logistics, waste recovery management and product recovery, and the triple bottom line concept which includes green logistics, environmentally conscious manufacturing and industrial ecology. The first concept aims at the coordination of forward and reverse flows and thereby making the supply chain more environmentally friendly. The second concept, also known as the Triple E concept (economy, ecology and equity) has its focus on the forward supply chain whereby the optimization of the processes has to consider all three dimensions. Again, it is required that existing models are adapted to the new objectives.

Corbett and Klassen (2006) relate the development of environmental (operations) management to the developments which have taken place in quality and supply chain management. Both streams had a huge impact on the operations management community by broadening its perspective. For instance, ideas from quality management are closely related to environmental protection (see, e.g., quality and environmental management standards by ISO, 2010). But the question of how environmental performance is defined and measured has not yet been clearly answered.

Linton et al. (2007) relate environmental sustainability and supply chains in their work. They state that focusing on the whole supply chain can significantly contribute to sustainability. Furthermore, supply chains have to be extended to include by-products of the supply chain; the entire life cycle of the product has to be considered and the optimization has to be done based on total cost which includes the effects of resource depletion and the generation of by-products, such as pollutants and waste. Sustainability is a topic which relates to both, natural and social sciences and is linked by policy-making. The relationship between policy and operations and supply chain management is evident. Policies impose restrictions on supply chains which have to be considered in decision-making, whereas the latter can affect policy and science by presenting alternative ways of operating and innovations.

As shown by the literature review many conceptual papers about how to integrate environmental issues into supply chain management are available whereby most of them point out the need for extending "traditional" supply chain management by considering the impact of supply chain activities on the environment. In addition to that lots of work can be found which covers the issue of reverse logistics and closed-loop supply chains. To the best of our knowledge, less work has been done with respect to the forward supply chain, its impacts on the environment and how to integrate environmental issues and regulations into decision-making. With our work we want to contribute to this new and emerging field of research.

2.4 Carbon emissions resulting from supply chain activities

Supply chains have various impacts on the environment by, for instance, consuming natural resources and producing waste or emissions that negatively affect the environment. Life-cycle assessment is a method for gathering data on environmental impacts of products and their supply chain processes. It is used for the systematic evaluation of the effects which a product has on the environment over the entire period of its life. In the broadest sense the term life-cycle refers to a "cradle-to-grave" approach considering sourcing, production, transportation, usage and post-usage phase. A "cradle-to-gate" analysis represents a partial life cycle assessment whereby it takes into account all the upstream processes of the product's life cycle until it is manufactured and reaches the factory gate (ISO, 2010). Guidelines for conducting a life-cycle assessment can be found in the ISO 14 000 series of the International Organization for Standardization (ISO, 2010), the related guidelines PAS 2050 (BSI Group, 2010) and the handbook for the International Reference Life Cycle Data

System (European Commission, 2010b). By doing a life-cycle assessment the environmental impact of a product and the related supply chain processes can be measured and the results can be used for restructuring the supply chain processes or implementing new technologies in order to reduce the negative environmental impact (Hagelaar and van der Vorst, 2002).

A life cycle assessment consists of four phases, i.e. the definition of the goal and scope, the life cycle inventory analysis (data gathering), the impact assessment and the interpretation of the results (ISO, 2010). The first key element is to identify and quantify the environmental loads involved, such as the energy and raw materials consumed, the emissions and wastes generated. Several different methods can be applied for the life cycle inventory analysis (Suh and Huppes, 2005). As secondary data sources, life cycle inventory databases can be used which contain reference values for different products (see, for instance, Ecoinvent, 2011). Then, it is necessary to evaluate the potential environmental impacts of these loads and to assess the options available for the reduction of the environmental impacts. Environmental impacts include, for example, global warming/climate change, acidification, eutrophicaton or ecotoxicity (European Commission, 2010b).

Climate change, as one of the impact categories of a life-cycle assessment, is one of the biggest issues in today's world and carbon emissions are considered to be one of the key factors intensifying global warming (IPCC, 2007). Therefore, especially the carbon footprint of products has become more important in recent years. The carbon footprint represents a sub-set of the data covered by a life cycle assessment. The carbon footprint is a measure of the total amount of carbon dioxide equivalent (CO_2e) emissions (in grams, kilograms or tons) that is directly and indirectly caused by an activity or is accumulated over the life stages of a product. The carbon footprint contains not only carbon dioxide emissions but also emissions of other greenhouse gases, such as CH_4, N_2O and SF_6 (Wiedmann and Minx, 2008). In order to sum up these gases to the single indicator CO_2e conversion factors have to be applied in order to represent the difference in the global warming potential of the greenhouse gases (IPCC, 2007).

The carbon footprint includes the carbon emission related to production, warehousing as well as transportation processes. In this respect, a distinction between direct and indirect emissions has to be made; direct emissions result from the combustion of fossil fuels while indirect emissions are associated with energy use and therefore, depend on the way the energy is produced (Wiedmann and Minx, 2008). The importance of a certain stage decisively depends on the product under investigation and the respective supply chain. In order to get a complete carbon footprint a life cycle assessment is necessary which requires a huge amount of resources, time and expertise for gathering and analysing the detailed process data. Instead of a life cycle assessment, very recently analytical models for determining the carbon footprint of supply chains have been developed (Sundarakani et al., 2010) whereby the results still have to be validated with real-world data. The carbon footprint of a product is directly related to the supply chain carbon efficiency which is the quantity of products produced divided by the total amount of carbon emissions. According to Craig et al. (2009) this ratio can be used as a new performance measure in the evaluation of supply chains and by reducing the product carbon footprint the carbon efficiency of a supply chain is automatically improved.

The (product) carbon footprint also receives increasing attention from the customer's side and can therefore be used for marketing purposes. Several initiatives with respect to carbon labelling aim at showing the carbon content of a certain product in order to influence the customer's product choice. In order to guarantee a reasonable application of such labels standardized procedures for measuring carbon emissions from supply chain processes still have to be developed (Halldorsson et al., 2009). There are different kinds of carbon labels, namely carbon labels showing the absolute amount of carbon emissions of a product during its life cycle, carbon intensity labels, carbon rating labels, carbon reduction labels and carbon neutral labels. These labels serve different purposes as a marketing instrument and display different kinds of information. And at the moment it is sill doubted that carbon labels encourage a "greener" product choice of customers; they might rather lead to confusion of customers (Walter and Schmidt, 2008).

Beside the product's carbon footprint, the emissions resulting from transport activities are in the focus of political debates on the European level. The carbon emissions from the transport sector within the EU-27 are the only ones which have grown significantly between 1990 and 2006 with an increase of 26%. Carbon emissions from international aviation and navigation have witnessed an even stronger increase of 102% and 60%, respectively, between 1990 and 2007. Furthermore, in 2007, transport (excluding international aviation and maritime navigation) accounted for almost 20% of carbon emissions within the EU and therefore was the second largest polluter behind heavy energy-intensive industries (EEA, 2008, 2009).

For determining the carbon emissions from transportation processes, carbon emission calculators have been developed. These calculators help to quickly determine the carbon emissions resulting from transportation activities based on several input parameters, such as transport mode and vehicle type used, distance travelled, load factor and type of product (weight and volume). But these transport carbon calculators differ very much with respect to the parameters such transport modes included and the geographical scope. Mtalaa et al. (2009) present an overview of carbon emission calculation models and

Treitl et al. (2010) show how a state-of-the-art carbon calculator for transport could be integrated with transportation management systems which are used for planning and controlling purposes.

Beside such tools which can be applied on the company level, the determination and forecast of the total carbon footprint which results from freight transport is an important issue. Piecyk and McKinnon (2010) use six factors which influence the freight transport carbon footprint to develop scenarios for the development of the UK road transport and the related carbon emissions by 2020. These factors are structural factors related to the number, location and capacity of factories, warehouses and other facilities in a supply chain, commercial factors which determine companies' sourcing and distribution strategies and policies, operational factors which influence the product flow and functional factors which are related to the management of the transport. In addition to that, product-related factors, such as the packaging and the design of products affect the nature of the transport operation, and external factors, such as regulations, macro-economic trends and technology improvements, have to be considered. Most of these factors are directly related to supply chain management decisions which underlines the importance of these decisions for transport carbon emissions.

2.5 Environmental regulations impacting supply chain decisions

Environmental regulations are implemented by national governments or international bodies. These regulations aim at reducing the negative impact of economic activities on the environment and tackle problems, like global warming, depletion of natural resources or declining biodiversity. Of course, these regulations also have an impact on supply chains. Especially climate change is a global problem and therefore has to be tackled by global agreements, such as the Kyoto Protocol. The aim is to achieve economic growth while at the same time assuring environmental protection. But especially for developing countries other challenges, such as poverty or social unrest, might be more eminent. Therefore, a global agreement on common actions is difficult to achieve (The World Bank, 2008).

2.5.1 Overview of environmental regulations

According to Coase (1960) the core of an efficient market is that each subject is confronted by the total costs and utilities of its activities. This is not the case if the production or utility function of a subject also contains parameters which are influenced by one or more other subject(s). These influencing parameters are denoted as positive or negative external effects. For instance, the external effects of transport are mainly negative ones. It is assumed that the negative externalities of transport impose costs upon the society, distinguishing between external costs of the infrastructure and external costs of the transport activity itself. The first includes mainly costs due to land use and soil sealing. The second comprises the costs of accidents, congestion, noise, air pollution and climate change due to carbon emissions. Further, external effects can be subdivided into psychological, pecuniary and technological externalities. In the case of externalities the private cost or utility are not in line with the social cost or utility and the resources are allocated in an inefficient way. Authorities try to increase the efficiency in the market with the help of policy measures aiming at the internalization of external costs (Eisenkopf, 2008).

Nagurney (2000) differs between demand-side and supply-side oriented environmental (policy) instruments. Supply-side oriented instruments include measures taken under technology and infrastructure (network design) policies. Concerning demand-side oriented policies, environmental regulations based on "command and control" are used to impose restrictions on enterprises. These instruments have already been or are now replaced by approaches based on economic incentives. The most popular instruments are to impose taxes on and grant subsidies to polluters or to use tradable pollution permits. These permits, also called allowances or certificates, are given to the polluters by regulatory authorities in order to limit the total amount of pollution (e.g. emissions, water pollutants, etc.). The permits can then be traded among the enterprises included in the regulation.

Similar to that, The World Bank (2008) differs between regulatory measures, fiscal measures, market-based instruments and voluntary agreements to combat climate change. Regulatory measures include regulations, standards, directives and mandates. These measures are mainly implemented to encourage energy efficiency and the use of renewable energy; they are commonly used in many OECD countries. For instance, the EU member states have committed themselves to cover 20% of their energy needs from renewables by 2020 and a directive regulating the labelling of household appliances according to their energy efficiency was agreed in 1996. In addition to that, fiscal policies and measures, which include environmental taxes and subsidies, are introduced in order to achieve different environmental goals. Market-based measures, such as emission trading and the use of tradable renewable energy certificates, are increasingly used as they can help to decrease the cost of mitigating emissions. Also voluntary agreements are becoming more popluar at the moment. These agreements are negotiated directly between the authorities and the industry and they offer more flexibility to the companies than other measures.

In general, research about environmental policies has a longer tradition in economics. An overview of environmental policy analysis from a macroeconomic perspective is given in Nijkamp and van den Bergh (1997). Due to the scope of this work, Sections 2.5.2 and 2.5.3 deal with two policy instruments directed at the reduction of carbon emissions, i.e. emission taxes and emission trading, respectively.

2.5.2 Emission taxes

As already stated, a tax on polluting activities can be used in order to internalize the external costs of environmental degradation. This charge which has to be paid per unit of emission can also be called Pigouvian tax or effluent tax. By this, a cost is assigned to a former byproduct of the operations of companies and therefore, it should become part of companies' decision-making (Xepapadeas, 1992). Most works dealing with the modelling of emission taxes and its impact on the economy stem from the macroeconomic field. For instance, Verhoef et al. (1997) model production and emission taxes in a spatial price equilibrium model in order to show how these taxes affect production and trade in a network. They derive the optimal production and transport taxes so that emissions remain below a specified limit and welfare is maximized. In addition, it is shown that environmental transport policies conducted in isolation have indirect side-effects which can be positive or negative. In general, transport emission taxes lead to a reduction of transport activity and the related emissions. Whether the overall effect on the environment is positive or negative decisively depends on the difference of pollution from production of the regions under consideration. Only if the pollution from production is the same in the regions isolated transport emission taxes have the desired overall reduction effect.

Carbon or energy taxes which are based on the carbon or energy content of products are already used especially in Northern Europe where they are considered as an effective instrument. Already in the early 1990s, Finland, Sweden and Norway introduced taxes on the carbon content of fossil fuels. Of course, carbon tax rates vary largely across the countries and between sectors and also depending on the fossil fuel used. The effectiveness of this measure is to some extent reduced due to tax reductions, rebates, tax ceilings or exemptions which are also introduced by the respective countries (The World Bank, 2008).

In general, with the help of emission taxes the difference between private and social cost should be compensated in order to derive a socially-desirable level of output. For companies emission taxes are a financial incentive to reduce emissions and equate their marginal abatement costs with the tax level.

Therefore, a tax should be preferred to imposing (absolute) restrictions on emissions or mandating certain technologies because such policy measures do not encourage companies to reduce emissions below the prescribed limit or invest in innovations. Furthermore, emission taxes are revenue-raising environmental policies where the revenues can be used to cut other taxes. But as a disadvantage, emission taxes lack precision with respect to emission quantities. This means that it is difficult to reach a specified reduction target with the help of an emission tax. Only if the policy-maker has complete knowledge of the abatement cost function of companies the effect of an emission tax on the emission quantity could be anticipated with certainty (Hoel, 1998). A further argument against emission taxes is that emission taxes which are imposed on producers directly lead to a cost increase and are, therefore, harmful to economic performance and in particular to employment. But this statement is not fully supported by economic theory (Hoel, 1998, Schneider, 1998).

An emission tax applied to the transport sector would have to consider the various transport modes as they produce a different amount of emissions. Making the transport modes pay their full external costs would increase the costs of the more polluting transport modes dramatically. For instance, a study from the UK has shown that this would require a doubling of the taxes on road transport (Piecyk and McKinnon, 2007).

2.5.3 Emission trading

The basic idea of emission trading is that a quantified physical constraint is set in the form of emissions allowances, permits or credits. These allowances are distributed among the agents who then have the right to trade these allowances amongst each other. One fundamental condition for the effective operation of emission trading is scarcity of emissions allowances (Knoll and Huth, 2008). The allowances are sometimes referred to as "pollution rights" as the holders of the allowances have the right to harm the environment (Raux, 2004, 2010). Crocker (1966), Dales (1968) and Montgomery (1972) are one of the first dealing with the formalization of pollution permit markets. They provide evidence that with such a system environmental damages can be reduced while minimizing abatement costs for the players in the market. Goulder et al. (1999) states that emission permits are as cost-effective as emission taxes given that the permits are sold to the producers at their market price through, for instance, an auction. Similar to emission taxes, also emission trading is usually preferred to performance standards or technology mandates.

One characteristic of an emission trading scheme, as a market-based instrument, is that it leaves freedom to the companies on how to comply with the regulation. The decisions over which strategy to use or which technology to implement is left to the companies which best understand their business operations. Furthermore, an emission trading program requires an integrated approach from the companies which means that the emission reduction strategy has to become part of the overall business strategy. The system itself is easy to understand; a company simply has to hold enough emission allowances to match its emissions. Policy-makers just have to concentrate on monitoring and verifying emissions, tracking the transfer of emission allowances and assessing potential penalties without having to make detailed reviews of the company's processes as in the case of technical specifications. But the flexibility of the system also increases the complexity for companies with respect to which compliance strategy should be chosen. Furthermore, the companies need to know their internal abatement costs in order to make a reasonable decision about buying and selling of emission allowances (Kruger, 2008). It is assumed that with the help of this system the most cost-effective way of emission reduction is chosen. The companies with high abatement costs prefer to buy additional allowances whereas those with low abatement cost reduce their amount of pollution and are then able to sell the remaining allowances (Nagurney, 2000, Raux, 2004). OECD (2001) summarizes the following benefits of tradable pollution permits:

- Environmental effectiveness: Such a system guarantees environmental performance by addressing environmental impacts directly through the setting of goals or quantified physical limits. For that, the strict monitoring of these quantified parameters is necessary.
- Decentralized flexibility: The agents have flexibility in the choice of means in achieving the environmental objectives.
- Economic efficiency: It helps to minimize the overall cost of compliance by encouraging the agents that can abate pollution more cheaply to do so first, while allowing those with higher costs to opt for buying additional allowances.

At the moment, several (local) emission trading schemes covering greenhouse gas emissions are implemented worldwide. The EU emission trading scheme (EU ETS) is the largest of the currently valid schemes (Antes et al., 2008). The EU ETS came into force on January 1, 2005 based on a directive from 2003 (European Community, 2003b) and it imposes restrictions on companies with respect to the carbon emissions they produce measured in tons of CO_2e. The EU ETS was implemented in order to reach the goals stated in the Kyoto protocol. Frankly speaking, it resulted from the failure of the European Commission to introduce an effective EU-wide carbon energy tax and it was also preferred from an industry-perspective over "command and control" measures (Convery, 2009). It is a cap-and-trade system of allowances for emitting CO_2 and other greenhouse gases whereby each allowance certifies the right to emit one ton of CO_2e. Up to now, only certain industries are included in this regulation. These industries are mainly heavy energy-intensive industries. The EU ETS covers refineries, power generation with fossil resources, metal production and processing, pulp and paper and mineral industry. Today, more than 11,000 sites that produce around 40% of the EU's total CO_2e emissions are covered by the EU ETS. At the moment, most of the emission allowances are allocated to the companies free of charge via national allocation plans. Those companies that produce fewer emissions than the number of allowances owned can sell them, whereas those producing more than the assigned limit have to buy additional allowances, get credits by engaging in emission-saving projects (through clean development mechanisms or joint implementation projects) or have to pay a penalty. The aim is to reduce the number of allowances constantly, in order to decrease the total CO_2e emissions within the EU. The EU ETS is split into three trading periods; the first one ran from beginning of 2005 to the end of 2007, the second one lasts until the end of 2012 and the third one from 2013 to 2020 (European Community, 2005). During the first trading period, the market price for emission allowances witnessed a substantial decline due to oversupply (European Commission, 2006).

In 2007, the second largest "polluter" was transport accounting for nearly 20% (EEA, 2008). The EU is already planning to increase the number of companies and sectors which have to comply with the trading scheme, e.g. include civil aviation by 2012 (European Community, 2008). Beside the inclusion of additional sectors, also the mode of allocation will change in the future. At the moment, the allowances are allocated among the member states based on national allocation plans and then further distributed to the companies and the affected installations mostly free of charge. In the third trading period (2013-2020) more than half of the emission allowances will be auctioned intead of being allocatd for free (European Commission, 2010a). Furthermore, instead of the decentralized allocation of the emission allowances by each member state the allocation could be controlled by a central authority (Malueg and Yates, 2009).

In addition to that, the ETS directive (European Community, 2003b) foresees the linking of the European ETS with other national or regional emission trading schemes via international agreements. This should encourage the creation of a global emission trading scheme. So far, the major hindrance of linking the existing trading schemes is that they differ in their design features, such as coverage of sectors and emissions, which makes them incompatible. In addition to that, for a global emission trading scheme to emerge, first a global climate change agreement has to be reached (Egenhofer, 2007).

Raux (2010) claims that an emission trading scheme could be particularly appropriate for the transport sector because the agents in the transport sector are more sensitive to quantitative regulations than price signals, such as an emission tax. Furthermore, the acceptability of this instrument is higher compared to an additional tax and with this instrument the quantitative objective of emission reduction is guaranteed. But as a disadvantage high costs of administration may arise for the monitoring of the large number of mobile sources. While Perrels (2010) investigates the applicability of emission trading to passenger transport Raux (2010) analyse it for personal as well as for freight transport. In order to reduce administrative costs the emission trading system could be implemented at the upstream, where only a limited number of actors, such as fuel refiners or distributors, would be included in the emission trading. The disadvantage of this system is that the effect on the final emitter is very limited as for them it again results in an additional fee similar to a tax. In addition to that, considering free allocation of the allowances, the acceptability might suffer as those having to take effort for the reduction of emissions, namely the final emitters, do not benefit from the free allocation. In contrast to this, a downstream approach requires the monitoring and administration of a very large number of sources. Under a hybrid approach for emission trading fuel producers and vehicle manufacturers could be included. But this approach might also result in difficulties of, for instance, double counting. Under a downstream approach for freight transport, the most straightforward way is to target fossil fuel consumption as other potential targets, such as tonne-kilometres or vehicle-kilometres, are not easily accessible for regulators. Furthermore, logistics service providers or more specifically transport carriers could be the main parties involved in an emission trading for transport. But it has to be kept in mind that the carriers are limited in their actions by the requirements imposed by the shippers. So in order to guarantee the effectiveness of the systems the shippers have to be involved as well, especially when they carry out the transport themselves. Raux (2010) suggests that any freight vehicle user needs to present the necessary allowances at the time of fuel purchase. The transfer of allowances between transport carriers and shippers can become part of the contractual relationship and the trade of allowances would be based on a stock market.

Overall, emission trading can be a cost-effective measure to reduce carbon emission to a predefined level set by authorities also in the transport sector. But in order to achieve the desired effects and to not cause disadvantages for certain countries or regions emission trading has to be implemented on a global scale as argued by Sinn (2009).

Chapter 3

Integrating the environmental dimension into supply chain decisions

Basically, the environment can be integrated into decision-making by adding (a) constraint(s), by monetarisation of the environmental impact and including it in the cost or profit function or by using multi-objective programming approaches. We present the existing work grouped according to different supply chain decisions. For our purpose, these are network design decisions, inventory (ordering) decisions, production mix and production planning decisions and transport mode and transport planning decisions. Within each section we describe the different works and point out similarities and disparities. Section 3.5 provides a summary of the presented models and underlines the relations to our work.

3.1 Network design decisions

Hugo and Pistikopoulos (2005) develop a multi-objective optimization model for network design and apply it to a case from the chemicals industry. Beside a classical economic criterion, i.e. maximizing net present value, the minimization of the impact of the network on the environment is included in the objective function. The decisions to be taken include the location and capacity of facilities and the establishment of transportation links in order to be able to supply the markets. Based on the idea of life cycle assessment the environmental impacts of the different stages are considered, i.e. the extraction of raw materials, the production of the final goods, the transportation of raw materials and final goods and the supply of the plants with utilities. These impacts are aggregated to a single environmental indicator called Eco-Indicator 99 (Goedkoop and Spriensma, 2001). In their model, there is a clear trade-off between minimizing environmental impact and maximizing net present value. The solution to this problem is a set of efficient or pareto-optimal solutions whereby each solution represents an alternative supply chain design option with corresponding environmental and economic performance. The two extreme solutions represent the supply chain design with minimum environmental impact or maximum net present value, respectively. A similar approach is taken by Bojarski et al. (2009) who also include an aggregated environmental indicator (IMPACT2002+, see, Jolliet et al., 2003) to sum-up various environmental impacts of the supply chain. The environmental impact is balanced with the costs resulting from a certain supply chain design. In addition to that, emission trading is considered in the model formulation but in their case study, the consideration of emission trading does not have an impact on the network design decision.

Also, Quariguasi Frota Neto et al. (2008) argue that, nowadays, in the design of logistics networks in addition to cost minimization also the minimization of environmental impacts has to be included. They develop a framework for designing and evaluating sustainable logistics networks in which costs and environmental impacts are balanced with a multi-objective programming approach. As in Hugo and Pistikopoulos (2005) and Bojarski et al. (2009) the multi-objective approach helps to determine the trade-offs between these two performance indicators. They introduce the term "pareto-optimal frontier" which is related to the concept of eco-efficiency (Huppes and Ishikawa, 2005). The pareto-optimal frontier is defined by the set of extreme points of the multi-objective program. This means that for each supply chain configuration which lies on the efficient frontier it is not possible to decrease costs without increasing environmental impact and vice versa. The efficient frontier serves as benchmark for existing networks. They extend the work of Bloemhof-Ruwaard et al. (1996) who analyse the impact of different recycling scenarios in a network model in the European pulp and paper industry. They consider the forward and reverse supply chain and evaluate the impact of recycling quotas on the network and the associated costs and emissions. It turns out that too high mandatory recycling quotas are not environmentally friendly. Based on this work, Quariguasi Frota Neto et al. (2009b) further develop the framework for sustainable logistics networks and the issue of assessing eco-efficiency with the help of multi-objective programming. They apply it to a closed-loop supply chain, more specifically to the German electronics industry, and consider the WEEE directive, which is a regulation on waste from electrical and electronic equipment (European Community, 2003a). The cumulative energy demand on the different supply chain stages and the waste produces are taken as criteria to measure the environmental performance. As conclusion they point out that by implementing a closed-loop supply chain, which takes care of the waste products, it does not necessarily lead to a supply chain with low environmental impact measured by the cumulative energy demand.

Cruz (2008), Cruz and Wakolbinger (2008), Cruz and Matsypura (2009) take the concept of corporate social responsibility (CSR) which includes among others the aim for environmental preservation and integrate it in a multi-period network design model consisting of manufacturers, retailers and consumers. By investing in corporate social activities the amount of emissions due to production and transport and the level of risk can be reduced. The manufacturers' and retailers' objectives are maximizing total profit, minimizing total emissions and minimizing risk. Those three objectives are combined into a single objective function by assigning weights to each part. The consumers make their decisions depending on the product prices and the transaction costs. They derive the optimality conditions for all three parties assuming that they act non-cooperatively. The network is in equilibrium when all optimality conditions hold and no decision maker is better of by altering his/her decision. With numerical examples it is shown that higher costs for the corporate social activities lead to lower levels of CSR and a reduction of product flows. Cooperation within the supply chain, which is the coordination of CSR activities in this work, would help to improve the performance of the whole supply chain.

A network design model which also considers the carbon emissions related to production and transportation is developed by Ramudhin et al. (2008). They analyse the impact of a cap-and-trade system for emission allowances on the network design decisions. Therefore, in the economic objective function in addition to the fixed costs of facilities, the fixed costs for assignment of products and raw materials, fixed shipment costs, and variable supply and transportation costs also the emission costs or gains are included. Alternatively, multi-objective programming is used and the minimization of carbon emission is also considered in the objective function. They apply the model to a case from the steel industry and specifically analyse the impact of different transport modes on carbon emissions. By using the multi-objective approach a comparably good solution with respect to costs and carbon emissions can be achieved in contrast to a pure economic or environmental optimization.

Diabat and Simchi-Levi (2009) develop a network design model with a carbon cap whereby emissions stem from three sources, namely from plants depending on the consumed energy, from warehouses depending on the volume in stock and from distribution due to the travelled distance between facilities. The supply chain costs consist of shipping costs for transport between plants, warehouses and customers and fixed facility costs for operating plants and warehouses. With a numerical example of a two-level multi-commodity facility location problem they show that a decreasing carbon cap leads to an increase of the supply chain costs. Their work is extended by Abdallah et al. (2010) who consider in addition to the carbon cap the possibility of buying or selling carbon credits. Thereby, additional costs incur if the carbon cap is violated or revenues can be generated by selling excess carbon credits. Furthermore, they distinguish a set of suppliers which differ depending on the carbon emissions embedded in the raw materials. Beside the emissions from the raw materials, emissions also stem from transport (from suppliers, between plants and distribution centres and to customers), energy used in production and the volume stored in the distribution centres. The supply chain costs are the same as in Diabat and Simchi-Levi (2009) extended by the procurement costs (unit raw material costs and shipping costs of the raw materials) and the carbon trading costs. With numerical analyses they show that with increasing carbon costs the total carbon emissions of the supply chain decrease. The total costs first increase because carbon credits are bought due to their low price instead of improving carbon efficiency. But at a certain point, i.e. as soon as the abatement costs are lower than the carbon costs, the total supply chain costs decrease. In addition to that, it is shown that the number of distribution centres increase with higher carbon costs as it is reasonable to reduce transport distances in order to keep the emissions from transport low.

In the field of network design models, several works with an multi-objective programming approach can be found whereby the goal of these models is to specify the trade-off curve between economic and environmental criteria. Other works simply extend "classical" network design models by including emission taxes as additional costs in the objective function or by adding an additional constraint limiting the amount of emissions which result from production, inventory and transportation.

3.2 Inventory (ordering) decisions

In recent works, Bonney (2009) and Bonney and Jaber (2010) underline the importance of extending classical models of inventory management to also account for the environmental impacts. This should help to design responsible inventory systems which are systems also reflecting the needs of the environment. They present an overview of potential environmental problems related to inventory and list environmental performance metrics for inventory systems. Several open questions about the impact of inventory systems are pointed out, like, what are the effects of the different replenishment rules on the environment, how does the number and location of inventory facilities impact the energy used in transportation or how does the design of a storage area affect the energy use? A comprehensive work about the relation between inventory and energy is provided by Zavanella and Zanoni (2009). Further, Bonney and Jaber (2010) underline that several developments of the past, such as just-in-time delivery, might be reconsidered if the environmental effects are taken into account. As a first step of integrating inventory systems and the environment, they extend the economic order quantity model to show how the environmental dimension could be integrated in existing models. Even though the modelling is quite straightforward the interpretation of the results has to be done carefully. In addition to the classical cost parameters, i.e. fixed ordering costs, purchasing costs and holding costs per unit, they include transportation costs for delivered and returned items and emissions costs from transportation. In addition, they assume that a certain amount of the order quantity has to be disposed of for which disposal costs arise. They conclude that in the environmentally-extended economic order quantity model the optimal order quantity is larger than in the classical model whereby the difference decisively depends on the value of the parameters.

In line with this approach, Hua et al. (2011) also use the economic order quantity model and extend it with carbon emissions from inventory holding and transport. They examine the impacts of carbon trading, a carbon price and a carbon cap on the optimal order quantity, carbon emissions and total cost. So they are able to evaluate the impact of regulations on a company's decision. The emissions from inventory are included in the model with a factor representing the amount of variable emissions due to holding a product unit in stock. A fixed amount of carbon emissions is associated with each order which, therefore, stands for the emissions from transport. They put a carbon price on the emissions from inventory holding and transport. Thereby, emissions are transformed into a markup on the inventory holding costs and on the fixed ordering costs. Also a carbon cap is considered in the extended total cost function. With the extended model the optimal order quantity for the classical model, assuming a carbon price of zero, can be calculated as well as the order quantity resulting in the lowest emissions. The optimal order quantity is independent of the carbon cap but decisively depends on the carbon price and the relation between the emission ratio (variable emissions from inventory holding divided by fixed emissions) and the cost ratio (variable holding costs divided by fixed ordering costs). If these two ratios are equal, the extended model yields the same result as the classical model and the resulting order quantity minimizes costs and emissions at the same time. If the emission ratio is greater than the cost ratio, the optimal order quantity is smaller than the classical optimal order quantity, and vice versa. They conclude that if the emissions from inventory holding are relatively large compared to the emissions from transport the decision maker should keep less inventory by choosing a small order quantity. While this conclusion is straightforward the impact on the total costs is not. They derive critical values for the carbon cap and the carbon price and their impact on the total costs. As long as the carbon cap is smaller than the minimal emissions, i.e. the emissions resulting from the order quantity which minimizes the emissions, the total costs are always greater than the total costs in the classical economic order quantity model. In other words, if the decision maker has to buy carbon credits, the total costs are bound to increase. But if the decision maker is able to sell carbon credits, the total costs may increase or decrease. A reduced carbon cap – given a fixed carbon price – does not affect the optimal order quantity and the resulting carbon emissions, but total costs increase because more carbon credits have to be bought. If the carbon price increases – given a fixed carbon cap – the order quantity remains constant, increases or decreases depending on the relation between emission ratio and cost ratio. Two thresholds and the carbon cap determine the impact of an increasing carbon price on the total cost. If the cap is smaller than a threshold, the total costs increase; if the cap is greater than another threshold the total costs decrease. And if the carbon cap is between the thresholds the total costs first increase and then decrease with increasing carbon price. To conclude, the cap-and-trade mechanism induces the decision maker to reduce carbon emissions which may result in higher costs. But under some conditions, carbon emissions and total costs can be reduced simultaneously.

Benjaafar et al. (2010) also investigate to which extent carbon emissions can be reduced by operational adjustments in procurement, production and inventory management without investing in carbon-reducing technologies. They argue that business practices and operational policies might have a larger impact on carbon emissions than technological improvements. Furthermore, lacking coordination within supply chains also creates "carbon inefficiencies" and a higher carbon footprint. They build their analyses on (dynamic) lot-sizing models for single and multiple firms and incorporate different policy settings in the basic models, namely emission caps, emission taxes, emission trading and carbon offsets. The single firm model is similar to the one proposed by Hua et al. (2011) whereby the decision maker's problem is when and how much to order (produce) over a fixed planning horizon consisting of multiple periods with known demand. The objective without consideration of carbon emissions is to minimize the sum of the fixed and variable ordering (production) costs, inventory holding costs and shortage costs. In their framework, fixed carbon emissions are associated with each order; in addition, they consider variable emissions per unit ordered and variable emissions per unit of inventory. The total emissions increase linearly in the associated decision variables. Depending on the policy setting, emissions are either modelled as a constraint (carbon cap), as part of the cost function (emission tax) or both (emission trading and carbon offsets). They extend the single-firm model to multiple firms with and without collaboration. Based on numerical sensitivity analyses they provide conclusions for the different models. For the single-firm model with a carbon cap they conclude that meaningful caps can have a large impact on emission reductions without a high increase of total costs. From sensitivity analyses of different emission factors the impact of technological improvements can be investigated and in their setting changing operational practices turns out to be more cost-efficient than investing in new technologies. Tighter caps can be implemented without negative impact on costs when it is allowed to use carbon offsets to meet the emission constraint. So from a business point of view, economic incentives to reduce carbon emissions are more reasonable than simple restrictions on emissions. Similar to Hua et al. (2011) they conclude that under a cap-and-trade system the emission levels are not affected by the cap but only by the emission price. Therefore, the impact of a cap-and-trade system on the total carbon emissions is similar to an emission tax and a lower carbon cap only indirectly reduces total emission via a higher carbon price. The numerical analyses of the multiple-firm model show that carbon regulations increases the value of collaboration whereby collaboration is particularly beneficial under a strict carbon cap. But the collaboration might not be beneficial for all firms, so contractual agreements are needed in order to create a win-win situation for all firms involved. Finally, they point out that supply chain-wide emission caps have the potential to reduce emissions and costs at the same time.

In contrast to the two models presented above which assume deterministic demand Chen and Monahan (2010) incorporate environmental issue in a stochastic multi-period inventory and production model. They examine the impact of regulatory and voluntary pollution control policies on a firm's inventory decision and on the environment. In their framework, waste is produced as byproduct of the primary production process. A pollution index represents the amount of waste due to the production of one unit of the primary product. This index is not a constant but assumed to be a random variable in order to reflect the uncertainty of the production process and the resulting amount of waste or emissions. In addition to that, demand is also modelled as a random variable. An environmental standard imposes restrictions on the number of products that can be produced by the firm whereby this standard can be regulatory or voluntary. It has to be kept in mind that due to the uncertainty of the pollution index also the environmental limit is uncertain. Under a regulatory pollution control approach, the firm is not allowed to violate the pollution limit whereas under the voluntary pollution control approach, the firm can exceed the limit in the case of product shortages. They show that the mandatory pollution limit induces the firm to produce more in order to cope with the uncertainty; an environmental safety stock is kept in order to prepare for a possible shortage in the future when the environmental standard restricts the optimal production quantity. Under the voluntary environmental standard the firm can exceed the environmental limit but there is a penalty cost per each excess unit of waste. In this way, the environmental consideration is internalized into the decision-making process of the firm. It is shown that the production level and together with it the environmental safety stock is lower than under the regulatory environmental standard and results in better environmental performance. This work also provides insights for policy-making by showing that a strict policy does not automatically lead to a better environmental performance.

All the works found in the field of inventory management relate to the impact of environmental regulations on the inventory decision. For the economic order quantity model it is concluded that regulations with respect to emissions from transport, generally, result in a larger order quantity; but it is also pointed that if also emissions for carrying inventory are considered, the impact on the order quantity depends on the ratio between the emission and the cost factors. Furthermore, in most works it is pointed out that in the case of emission trading the optimal decision is independent of the imposed emission limit. It is interesting that, even though inventory is only rarely affected by environmental regulations, in this field such regulations are already considered in research.

3.3 Production mix and production planning decisions

One of the first works which integrates environmental regulations in production control is Dobos (1998) based on the works of Wirl (1991) and Wirl (1995). Pollution charges and constraints are integrated into the Holt-Modigliani-Muth-Simon model (Holt et al., 1960) which is one the of the basic models for aggregate production planning. The pollution and the related charges depend on the production level. It is shown that a linear charge reduces the production rate and the inventory level; a quadratic pollution charge leads to a smoother production rate and a lower inventory level. In general, a pollution constraint imposes an additional constraint on the production decision and therefore, reduces the range of production possibilities which has already been shown by Wirl (1991, 1995).

Penkuhn et al. (1997) present an optimization model for production planning in the process industry and integrate byproducts, residues and emission taxes. The model is applied to a case study from the chemical industry (an ammonia synthesis plant for the production of fertilizers). The major environmental concerns of the production process are emissions from the combustion of the fuel gas, the consumption of cooling water and the energy used. In order to represent the high complexity of the production process a non-linear optimization problem is formulated. The objective is to maximize the profit margin by deciding upon the material flow. In addition to the classical objective function, costs for recycling and disposal of emissions and waste are integrated into the objective function. Also, additional constraints representing environmental issues are incorporated, namely the maximum amount of waste going to landfill and the maximum amount of emissions. They show that their integrated approach leads to a slight improvement of the profit of the production process and a substantial reduction of energy use and direct emissions.

Letmathe and Balakrishnan (2005) formulate two mathematical models for production planning where the environment is explicitly considered in the decision. Both models can be used to determine the optimal product mix and production quantities while keeping different environmental constraints in addition to the typical production constraints. They pay special attention to the emissions produced during the production process. The regulations concerning emissions are taxes or penalties based on the produced output, fixed thresholds and the trading of emission allowances. The first model which is a linear program assumes that the operating procedure in order to produce a product is fixed in advance. The operating procedure defines the resources needed, the production yield and the emissions resulting from the production process. So the model is used to decide which products to produce and in which quantities. The objective is to maximize profits which consists of the revenues from product sales and selling of emission allowances less the production costs, the costs for the purchase of emission allowances and emission penalties. They assume that the purchasing price of emission allowances is higher than the selling price, mainly due to transaction costs. Three different emission constraints are formulated. The absolute emission constraint limits the total amount of emissions in a certain time period; the product-based emission constraint imposes an upper bound on the average amount of emissions produced based on the total production quantity; the resource-based emission constraint imposes an upper bound on the average amount of emissions of a specific resource. Furthermore, the demand function is related to the emission quantities by assuming that it decreases linearly depending on the amount of emissions produced. In the second model, each product can be produced using different operating procedures and in this case it also has to be decided which (combinations of) operating procedures are used, beside the product mix and the production quantities. This leads to a mixed integer program. With numerical analyses they provide insights into the impact of environmental regulations on the firm's decision and the performance of the firm. It is shown that the emission constraints affect the product mix. For instance, products with a negative profit margin but a low emission factor might be produced in order to help to keep the resource-based emission limit. The effect of emission trading mainly depends on the difference between the purchasing and the selling price of emission allowances. In the case of a high difference, (nearly) no trading takes place and emission trading has the same effect as a fixed emission limit. In the case of no difference between the two emission prices, emission trading has similar impacts as emission taxes.

Radulescu et al. (2009) formulate a multi-objective program for production processes in which they integrate constraints on (pollution) emissions. The decision maker can invest a certain amount of money in the production of different products while aiming at maximizing the expected return and minimizing the pollution risk. The risk is measured in monetary terms as pollution penalties. It is assumed that the emissions related to the production of one unit is not a constant but a random variable. For each type of emission they define three different levels (target/desirable, alarm and maximum level) and they consider two approaches of measuring environmental risk. The penalties which have to be paid are either proportional to the expected amount of pollutant that exceeds the level or proportional to the probability that the threshold is violated. Furthermore, they model environmental constraints differing between mean-type and safety-first environmental constraints. The mean-type environmental constraint limits the expected amount of emissions whereas the safety-first environmental constraint is related to the probability that the emissions exceed the limit. The model is a stochastic multi-objective programming problem for which they present several solution approaches and they apply the model to a case from the textile industry.

A large body of literature deals with the integration of remanufacturing in the classical lot-sizing model (see, for instance, Mabini et al., 1992, Golany et al., 2001, Minner and Lindner, 2004, Teunter, 2001, 2004, and the references therein). Remanufacturing means that instead of virgin material returned items are used in order to produce new items. The use of returned items helps to reduce costs, the use of raw materials and the production of waste. Furthermore, it is assumed that the production of remanufactured items can be more energy-efficient (Guide et al., 2000). So, these models generally assume that by applying remanufacturing an improvement of the environmental dimension is achieved. Only a limited number of these works explicitly consider environmental criteria in decision-making. One of these is the work from Quariguasi Frota Neto et al. (2009a) who not only consider the costs but also the cumulative energy demand of (re)manufacturing. With the help of multi-objective programming they derive the pareto-efficient frontier which shows the trade-off between costs and energy demand. From that it can be derived which costs have to be accepted in order to achieve a certain environmental improvement.

Subramanian et al. (2010) develop a non-linear mathematical programming model which they apply to the field of engine (re)manufacturing. Beside presenting the modelling approach, they highlight the information requirements in order to provide reliable decision support. The objective function is profit maximization and they include the environmental dimension on the different supply chain stages, i.e. product design, production and recovery. In product design, the environmental performance of the engine is set, which can be either the engines's emissions or fuel use, and the remanufacturability of an engine is determined. Both decisions are related to design costs which increase with higher performance and higher remanufacturability. In production, the firm has to decide how many quantities of new and remanufactured products should be produced as output. The new and remanufactured products have different (production, disposal, inventory and back-ordering) costs, compete for capacity, face different demand and produce different amounts of emissions. They consider emission limits and the selling and buying of emission allowances for the (re)manufacturing processes. The consideration of an emission limit has a significant impact on the product mix, namely the overall production level decreases and the level of remanufacturing increases due to the favourable emission factors of remanufactured engines.

Also simulation tools and scenario-based analysis can be used to design production processes under environmental considerations. Taplin et al. (2006) present a case study from the metal industry investigating different production processes. They model a supply chain including production, transportation and reverse flows of scrap metal which then can be recycled. They mainly show the impact of different production processes on energy consumption in production and carbon emissions from transport and conclude that under certain circumstances a reduction of negative environmental impact can be accompanied by cost reductions through improved efficiency.

The review shows that the consideration of the environment in decision-making in the field of production planning has a rather long tradition with works dating back to the early 1990s. This might be due to the fact that the (negative) impacts of production activities on the environment are evident and environmental regulations are often imposed on manufacturing installations. Different methods ranging from multi-objective programming to linear or mixed-integer optimization and simulation are applied in this field to integrate environmental criteria in decision-making.

3.4 Transport mode and transport planning decisions

Anciaux and Yuan (2007) present a model for transport mode choice based on cost minimization where the shipment costs consist of transportation, inventory and transshipment costs. The transportation costs include fixed costs of the transport modes as well as variable costs depending on distance and time. In addition to that, the volume and weight of the products related to the capacity of a transport mode are considered as constraints. The inventory costs depend on the number of products in transit and the transshipment costs vary by mode and depend on the number of transshipments. The environmental impact of the transport modes is split into three types, namely air emission, noise pollution and accident risk. With the help of these performance measures different transport modes can be compared and depending on the objectives of the decision maker the mode with the lowest cost or the lowest environmental impact can be chosen or the two dimensions can be integrated into a single objective function with weighting factors.

Related to this, Kim et al. (2009) use a multi-objective approach in order to show the trade-off between the freight transport costs and carbon emissions. They distinguish between an intermodal network and a truck-only network. The goal is to determine the freight modal split between road, rail and short sea shipping. Emissions stem from the transportation process as well as the transshipment points and are considered in the objective function besides the transportation costs. They apply their model to a network in Europe and derive the trade-off curves for this case study.

Cholette and Venkat (2009) analyse the environmental impact of different distribution options from a winery to the customers with the help of a web-based tool, called CargoScope. They do not provide decision support based on an optimization model but compare different distribution scenarios and their resulting emissions from transportation and storage. The scenarios range from long-distance transport by road, rail or air, to local distribution via a retailer and customer pick-up. They show that the results vary by up to a factor of eighty. Wineries should focus on minimizing carbon emissions from transport; those from warehousing are, in general, negligible, as wine does not require strict cooling. Transport carbon emissions can be reduced by improving transport efficiency through higher load factors or using more environmentally friendly modes. Similar conclusions have already been drawn by Venkat (2007) who shows with the help of several case studies that depending on the product characteristics, in particular cooling requirements, there can be a clear trade-off between emissions from transport and inventory.

te Loo (2009) presents a methodology for calculating carbon emissions from transport and evaluates the impact of emission regulations. Different actions, like the increase of the load factor or modal split, and their impact on carbon emissions reductions are evaluated. Modal shift proves to be an effective action leading to carbon emission reductions and a decrease of costs. In particular, different variants of including transport activities in the European emission trading scheme are investigated, such as including only a certain number of transport modes in the existing emission trading scheme or building a separate transport emission trading scheme. It is assumed that an emission trading scheme simply means that costs are associated with emitting carbon emissions. So, in this model, emission trading is assumed to being equal to a linear carbon emission tax not considering the specifics of selling and buying of emission allowances.

The work of Hoen et al. (2010) deals with the problem of transport mode choice and specifically does focus on how to derive emission factors for the different modes. In addition to that, the impact of regulations on the decision is evaluated. They consider an emission limit and a linear emission tax. A production facility receives items from a supplier and for the delivery different transport modes are available. The goal is to minimize the average cost per period and to decide which transport mode to use for the shipments. An order-up-to policy is assumed and the products are ordered periodically. Each transport mode has a unit transport cost and a deterministic supply lead time. The average cost consists of penalty cost, holding cost and transportation cost. The classical transport mode selection problem is extended by also considering the emissions from transport. Firstly, an emission-constrained problem is formulated which means that a fixed emission constraint limits the transport mode decision. In this case, the transport mode with the lowest minimum average cost which meets the emission constraint is selected. Secondly, an emission cost-minimization problem is formulated. For that purpose, emission costs are integrated into the original cost function. In addition to that, detailed emission factors for the different transport modes, air, rail, road and water are derived by considering the specifics of each transport mode and the product characteristics (weight and volume). From analytical and numerical analyses they conclude that regulations, like taxes or emission trading, are not effective in encouraging companies to use more environmentally friendly transport modes because the share of the transport costs in the total costs is too small. According to them a hard constraint on emissions would be much more effective.

Only recently practice and research have started to analyse the environmental impact of transport mode choice and transport planning decision on the environment. However, this research field seems to be fruitful in view of the stricter environmental regulations which might be imposed on the transport sector in the near future.

3.5 Summary of existing models and relation to this work

In Table 3.1 all the works presented are listed in alphabetical order and described according to the decision(s) taken and the approach(es) used. In addition to that, it is pointed out if environmental regulations are, explicitly, considered in the model(s) or not.

Works dealing with the impact of production on the environment have, according to our literature review, the longest tradition which might be due to the fact that production processes are often responsible for a large part of the negative environmental impacts of a product. More recently, several models dealing with the impact of network design decisions on the environment, in particular, on emissions from production and transport have been developed. Only a limited number of papers dealing with the impact of inventory decisions on the environment have been found. It is pointed out that this field of research seems to be fruitful and that improvements are expected from the incorporation of environmental aspects into inventory models. Furthermore, the modelling of the environmental impact of transport receives increasing attention nowadays because transport activities also contribute towards a large share to the total carbon emissions.

With our work we want to analyse the impact of sourcing and inventory (ordering) decisions on transport carbon emissions and investigate how different environmental regulations with respect to carbon emissions affect the decision-making of companies. We focus on the single-period dual sourcing model with an offshore and an onshore supplier based on the newsvendor framework (for more details see Chapter 4). With the help of this model order (and transport) quantities are determined. We integrate a strict emission limit for transport, a linear transport emission tax and emission trading in the classical model. For the modelling of the emission trading we rely on Letmathe and Balakrishnan (2005) assuming a difference between the buying and the selling price of emission allowances. Similar to Benjaafar et al. (2010) and Hua et al. (2011) who analyse deterministic inventory models, we investigate the impact of different environmental regulations on the optimal decision in a stochastic, single-period inventory model. Also the paper of Chen and Monahan (2010) is related to our work as they consider stochastic demand in a multi-period inventory and production model. In contrast to their model in which a stochastic pollution index is included to link the inventory/production quantity with emissions, we assume a constant (average) transport emission factor to point out the relation between offshore order quantity and transport carbon emissions. We also relate our work to the concept of pareto-efficiency (Quariguasi Frota Neto et al., 2008) and want to find out if there are regulatory conditions under which the economic performance can be improved without decreasing the environmental performance and vice versa.

To the best of our knowledge it is the first attempt to integrate environmental considerations and regulations in the dual sourcing decision. We think that our work helps to contribute to this new and emerging field of research by providing guidelines and implications for management and policy-making.

Table 3.1: Summary of existing models considering environmental performance of supply chains

Author(s)(Year)	Decision(s)	Modelling approach	Regulations
Abdallah et al. (2010)	Production and warehousing locations, production and transport quantities	As cost in the objective function and as constraint	Yes
Anciaux and Yuan (2007)	Transport mode	As cost in the objective function	No
Benjaafar et al. (2010)	Order quantity, inventory level, backorders	As cost in the objective function and/or as constraint	Yes
Bojarski et al. (2009)	Production and warehousing locations, selection of technology, production and transport quantities	Multi-objective programming	Yes
Bonney and Jaber (2010)	Order quantity	As cost in the objective function	Yes
Chen and Monahan (2010)	Inventory/production level (environmental safety stock)	As cost in the objective function and/or as constraint	Yes
Cruz (2008), Cruz and Wakolbinger (2008), Cruz and Matsypura (2009)	Production and transport quantities, product prices, level of corporate social responsibility	Multi-objective programming	No
Diabat and Simchi-Levi (2009)	Production and warehousing locations, production and transport quantities	As constraint	Yes
Dobos (1998)	Production plan	As cost in the objective function and/or as constraint	Yes
Hoen et al. (2010)	Transport mode	As cost in the objective function or as constraint	Yes
Hua et al. (2011)	Order quantity	As cost in the objective function and as constraint	Yes
Hugo and Pistikopoulos (2005)	Production locations, production and transport quantities	Multi-objective programming	No
Kim et al. (2009)	Transport mode, transport quantities	Multi-objective programming	Yes
Letmathe and Balakrishnan (2005)	Product mix, production quantities, operating procedure	As cost in the objective function and as constraint	Yes
Penkuhn et al. (1997)	Production quantities	As cost in the objective function and as constraint	Yes
Quariguasi Frota Neto et al. (2008)	Production quantities (from virgin or recycled material), waste quantities, transport quantities	Multi-objective programming	No
Quariguasi Frota Neto et al. (2009a)	Production quantities (lot-sizes for new and remanufactured items)	Multi-objective programming	No
Quariguasi Frota Neto et al. (2009b)	Recycling/production quantities, transport quantities	Multi-objective programming	No
Radulescu et al. (2009)	Production quantities	Multi-objective programming	Yes
Ramudhin et al. (2008)	Production locations, use of transport mode(s), production and transport quantities, use of suppliers	As cost in the objective function or multi-objective programming	Yes
Subramanian et al. (2010)	Product design (performance), product mix, production quantities, product prices	As cost in the objective function and as constraint	Yes
Wirl (1991, 1995)	Production plan	As cost in the objective function and/or as constraint	Yes

Chapter 4

The economic and environmental performance of dual sourcing

This chapter is the core of our work. In Section 4.1, the basics of inventory management and the newsvendor model, which is taken as the cornerstone of this work, are presented. In Section 4.2 we cover sourcing decisions and deal in detail with dual sourcing in the newsvendor context. Then, in Section 4.3, we present a transport-focused dual sourcing framework which is the general setting where the focal company, i.e. a retailer, has to make its decision(s). With the help of this framework the dual sourcing decision is related to transport activity and the carbon emissions produced. Section 4.4 covers the basic single-period dual sourcing model and its extensions concerning regulations on carbon emissions from transport. It demonstrates how the decision of a company is influenced by the different types of regulations. Furthermore, the impact on the economic and environmental performance of the company is analysed. Section 4.5 includes the numerical results with sensitivity analyses which help to gain further insights into the models. From the analytical models and the numerical analyses managerial implications as well as implications for policy-making are derived and summarized in Section 4.6.

4.1 Inventory management and the newsvendor model

The decision how much inventory to hold and how much to order from a certain source is very important in relation to traditional performance measures, such as cost or profit and customer service. In the literature various ways can be found to model this decision problem. These inventory models serve different purposes with respect to the decision support they can provide. An overview of inventory models can be found in various operations and supply chain management textbooks, like Cachon and Terwiesch (2009), Chopra and Meindl (2010), Nahmias (2009) or Silver et al. (1998). Basically, a distinction between deterministic and stochastic inventory models can be made. In the first type of models certainty of the considered parameters, such as demand, lead time and costs/prices, is assumed, while the second assumes uncertainty of some parameters. An overview of stochastic inventory models can be found in Porteus (2002). Furthermore, single-period and multi-period inventory models can be distinguished whereby this distinction relates to the storability of the products and the number of ordering decisions which can be taken during the planning horizon.

The focus of this work is on the single-period inventory model, which is also known as the newsvendor or the newsboy problem. One basic assumption of the newsvendor model is that a single ordering decision has to be made before the beginning of the selling season, i.e. before demand is known. Therefore, demand is assumed to be uncertain/stochastic. No additional orders are possible during the selling season due to restrictions, like long lead times and short selling seasons. After the selling period the product is of no or only little value or costs might arise for the disposal of the product. This model can be applied to products with a short life cycle or whose lead time is longer than the selling period (Khouja, 1999). Typical products are apparel goods, sporting and fashion items and perishable products. The classical newsvendor model is based on a two-stage supply chain consisting of the supplier or producer and the retailer who sells the product to the final customer. The basic idea is that the retailer has to decide how much to order before demand is known. When demand is realized there are two possible outcomes; either demand is smaller than or equal to the order quantity or demand is larger than the order quantity. In the first case, items remain unsold in stock and there is leftover inventory; in the second case, a part of demand can not be satisfied from stock and the retailer incurs lost sales. In the basic model, it is assumed that the decision maker is risk-neutral and the objective is to maximize expected profit. For that, the decision maker has to balance the costs of overstocking, which arise when products remain unsold after the selling period, and the costs of understocking, which represent the opportunity costs of not fulfilling a customer request (Silver et al., 1998).

In the model the following parameters are included: The random demand X is characterized by the distribution function F. The retailer sells the product at the selling price per unit p to the final customer and procures the product from the supplier for the product price per unit c. Leftover inventory at the end of the regular selling season has a salvage value per unit z. It is assumed that $p > c > z$. Table 4.1 gives an overview of the notation for the classical newsvendor model.

Then the random profit P_{cl} depends on the order quantity q and on the realized demand x (see, for instance, Khouja, 1999):

$$P_{cl}(q, x) = \begin{cases} p \cdot x - c \cdot q + z \cdot (q - x) & x \leq q \\ (p - c) \cdot q - (p - c) \cdot (x - q) & x > q \end{cases} \tag{4.1}$$

Table 4.1: Notation for the classical newsvendor model

p	selling price per unit
c	product price per unit
z	salvage value per unit
x	realized demand
X	random demand
F	demand distribution function
F^{-1}	inverse of demand distribution function
q	order quantity
q_{cl}^{*}	optimal order quantity in the classical newsvendor model
$P_{cl}(q, x)$	random profit depending on order quantity q and realized demand x
$P_{cl}(q)$	expected profit depending on order quantity q
c_o	cost of overstocking per unit
c_u	cost of understocking per unit
$E()$	expected value
$(x)^{+}$	$\max(x, 0)$

In the classical model, the cost of understocking per unit (c_u) is represented by the contribution margin per unit ($p - c$). In extensions to the classical newsvendor model shortage penalties are considered (see, for instance, Khouja, 1999). The cost of overstocking per unit (c_o) is due to the difference between the product price and the salvage value per unit ($c - z$) and represents sunk costs due to items which remain unsold in stock. The expected profit is given as follows:

$$P_{cl}(q) = E(p \cdot X + z(q - X)^{+} - c \cdot q - (p - c)(X - q)^{+}) \qquad (4.2)$$

whereby $E()$ represents the expected value and $(x)^{+}$ is $\max(x, 0)$.

In the classical newsvendor model the optimal order quantity q_{cl}^{*} is derived by maximizing the expected profit. The fixed costs of ordering are neglected in the basic model due to the fact that the order is carried out anyway. In extensions to the classical model, fixed ordering costs or set-up costs are considered. The concept of mismatch costs which are the costs which arise due to a misalignment between demand and supply is important in this model. The expected mismatch costs are the sum of the expected cost of understocking and expected cost of overstocking and arise due to the fact that demand in uncertain. The mismatch costs are the difference between the maximum profit, which is the profit under certainty, i.e. if expected demand is realized and is represented by $(p - c) \cdot E(X)$, and the expected profit under demand uncertainty. The mismatch costs therefore represent the loss in supply chain efficiency due to uncertain demand. By ordering the quantity which maximizes the expected profit, simultaneously, the expected mismatch costs are minimized (Cachon and Terwiesch, 2009). As shown in Khouja (1999) $P_{cl}(q)$ is a concave function and the optimality condition, also known as critical fractile or critical ratio, is given by the following expression (see, also, Silver et al., 1998, Cachon and Terwiesch, 2009, Chopra and Meindl, 2010):

$$F\left(q_{cl}^{*}\right) = \frac{c_u}{c_u + c_o} = \frac{p - c}{p - z} \tag{4.3}$$

The critical fractile corresponds to the cycle service level, which is defined as the probability that the demand during the selling period is smaller than or equal to the order quantity. In other words, the cycle service level is the probability that all customer orders can be fulfilled within a selling season. The cycle service level is a non-financial economic performance indicator which measures the product availability within a supply chain (Chopra and Meindl, 2010).

By taking the inverse of the demand distribution function (F^{-1}) the optimal order quantity can be determined:

$$q_{cl}^{*} = F^{-1}\left(\frac{p - c}{p - z}\right) \tag{4.4}$$

Overall, the newsvendor model is one of the basic models of inventory management which helps to understand fundamental trade-offs in inventory decisions and it is, therefore, taken as the cornerstone of this work.

In most applications of the newsvendor model it is assumed that demand can be described by a known probability distribution. But some works also try to solve the newsvendor model without relying on a specific demand distribution (Scarf, 1958). A review about the distribution-free newsboy problem is presented by Gallego and Moon (1993). Distribution-free means that the goal is to maximize expected profit against the worst possible distribution and thereby a lower bound for the expected profit is derived. Moon and Gallego (1994) also give a review about distribution-free procedures for multi-period models.

An overview of several extensions of the classical newsvendor model is presented by Khouja (1999). Some works deal with the consideration of different objectives, such as maximizing the probability of achieving a target profit or the use of utility functions (Lau, 1980, Sankarasubramanian and Kumaraswamy, 1983, Lau and Lau, 1988). Other works consider supplier pricing policies, like quantity discounts, and different retailer pricing policies, random yield and different states of information about demand. The classical newsvendor model also severs as basis for multi-echelon systems. A recent work summarizing various extensions of the newsvendor model is provided by Qin et al. (2011) whereby they focus on extensions regarding integration of price- or marketing-dependent demand, stock-dependent demand, supplier discounting schemes and risk attitudes of the decision maker. Different risk attitudes of the decision maker can be considered considered, whereby risk-averse and/or risk-seeking behaviour is assumed instead of risk-neutrality (see, for instance, Lau, 1980, Anvari, 1987, Chung, 1990, Eeckhoudt et al., 1995, Chen et al., 2007, Jammernegg and Kischka, 2007, 2009, Fichtinger, 2010). Further extensions of the newsvendor model deal with the issue of multiple products and capacity, like Zhang and Du (2010). In addition to that, several works consider a second ordering possibility in the newsvendor model, which can be considered as backup or emergency supply option. This helps to increase the product availability and to increase the expected profit by reducing the expected mismatch costs. Section 4.2.2 covers this field of research in detail.

4.2 Sourcing decisions

As already mentioned in Section 2.1 sourcing is one of the key drivers of the performance of a supply chain and present the link of a company to its suppliers (Chopra and Meindl, 2010). The decision to outsource a process, i.e. letting a third party carry out an activity, or to perform it in-house is directly related to this issue. Sourcing allows a firm to obtain the appropriate inputs, either in the form of raw materials, components or final products, to be able to deliver the desired products to the market (Burke Jr., 2005). Section 4.2.1 gives an overview of the basics of sourcing and the different sourcing strategies which can be used by companies. Section 4.2.2 deals with the dual sourcing concept and the application of the newsvendor model to support decision-making in this respect.

4.2.1 Overview of sourcing concepts

According to Burke Jr. (2005) a company's sourcing strategy consists of three interrelated decisions:

- Establish a supplier base,
- Select suppliers from the supplier base which will receive an order and
- Decide upon the quantity of goods to order from each supplier selected.

In order to become part of the supplier base a supplier has to fulfil the company's requirements with respect to quality, quantity, delivery and price.

Table 4.2: Overview of sourcing strategies

Number of suppliers	single
	dual/double
	multiple
Origin of supplier(s)	local (onshore)
	global (offshore)
Duration of supplier relation	long-term partnership
	short-term market transaction
Type of interaction	direct
	indirect

Then, out of the supplier base one or a few suppliers are selected for a certain order. Finally, the company has to decide how much to order from the respective supplier(s).

Sourcing strategies can be categorized according to the number of suppliers, the origin of the supplier(s), the duration of the supplier relationship and the type of interaction with the supplier(s). An overview of the different strategies is shown in Table 4.2.

By pursuing a single sourcing strategy a long-term relationship and trust can be built between the company and its supplier. This helps to reduce administrative burdens, such as quality controls, and allows collaboration in other areas, such as product development. But by relying on a single supplier, dependency is created which is related to high risk; in case of delivery failure of the single supplier the company might need to stop production and can not deliver the desired products to the market. Furthermore, due to the non-existence of competition the price of the single supplier might be high (Burke et al., 2007). In order to avoid the disadvantages of single sourcing companies can pursue a multiple sourcing strategy. Multiple sourcing is especially advantageous for the procurement of standard components where a certain quality can be guaranteed by anonymous suppliers. Multiple sourcing aims at increasing competition between the suppliers and thereby achieving a low price on the market (van Mieghem, 2008). Furthermore, multiple sourcing helps to reduce supply risk which is shown by, for instance, Berger et al. (2004). Between these two extreme strategies – single sourcing from one well-known supplier and multiple sourcing from several anonymous suppliers on the market – dual or double sourcing can be a reasonable option. Dual sourcing in most cases means that two suppliers are used whereby one dominates the other in terms of share, price, reliability and other criteria (Yu et al., 2009). Under a tailored dual sourcing strategy a certain amount of the demand, which can be called the base demand, is allocated to the cost-efficient supplier in advance of the selling period. The uncertain, volatile demand is then satisfied by a more flexible supplier, when needed, or even produced internally (van Mieghem, 2008). In contrast to this, double sourcing denotes sourcing from two suppliers which provide similar service and deliver a comparable quantity of the product.

Furthermore, a company can decide to source locally or globally. By procuring from a local supplier, a short lead time and flexible supply can be realized. A local supplier can also be denoted as onshore supplier. The term onshore can also be applied to in-house production whereby in this context onshore means that the production site delivers to the market where it is situated. In contrast to this, global sourcing means that components are procured from all over the world, usually in order to exploit low unit product costs. Furthermore, some raw materials might not be available in the respective market and therefore, there is no other option than to source globally. In this respect, the terms offshoring and outsourcing are very important. The term outsourcing has to be clearly distinguished from offshoring which is related to the movement of a production facility abroad without necessarily giving up ownership. In contrast to this, outsourcing refers to letting a third-party carry out an operation and is not related to the geographical location of the supply source. Consequently, offshore outsourcing means that the products are delivered from an external supplier located in a low-cost country to the market (van Mieghem, 2008). By sourcing from an offshore source a longer transport lead time and/or higher transport costs are accepted for the sake of lower product costs per unit. In recent years, the shift to offshore suppliers or production has increasingly been questioned because it involves high risk and hidden costs (Warburton and Stratton, 2002) as well as a drastic increase of transport (Cadarso et al., 2010). Furthermore, sourcing from low-cost countries might be related to material losses in transit which can be due to theft, quality problems or product decay (Sounderpandian et al., 2008). Also Platts and Song (2010) show for several case studies in the context of sourcing from China that the total costs are often underestimated in practice and thus, alternative sourcing strategies might be more reasonable.

4.2.2 Focus on dual sourcing

Dual sourcing can be used in order to achieve cost efficiency and responsiveness at the same time. As already stated, dual sourcing means that two different supply sources are used. In general, the first supply source is the cost-efficient, inflexible supply source. The second supply source is the flexible supplier which can deliver on short notice. But for this flexibility a premium has to be paid. These two supply sources need not be two distinct entities; it can be the same supplier with two delivery options. But often the first supplier is located far away from the market and has a long lead time, i.e. offshore supplier, whereas the second supplier is located close to the market and can provide a short delivery lead time, i.e. onshore supplier (see, for instance, Warburton and Stratton, 2005, Allon and van Mieghem, 2010).

One of the first works dealing with a concept which is related to dual sourcing is provided by Barankin (1961). He presents an inventory model with an emergency supply option. In the general case, there is a one period lead time (time lag) until the order arrives, but in emergency cases immediate delivery is possible. An emergency situation arises when the initial stock is below a certain level, then immediate delivery of a fixed quantity is carried out. The emergency supply is related to additional costs. The total cost function includes holding and penalty costs as well as the costs for emergency supply. If the emergency supply costs are large compared to the penalty costs no emergency delivery is allowed at all. For the other case, when emergency supply is a reasonable option, the optimal emergency level together with the optimal order quantities, i.e. the regular order quantity and the emergency order quantity, are derived.

Gallego and Moon (1993) and Khouja (1996) deal with the newsboy problem and the possibility to place a second order if the first order is not sufficient to satisfy demand. According to Gallego and Moon (1993) after placing the first order demand is observed and an additional order can be placed to fulfil any demand that is not satisfied by the first one. The second order is related to higher costs than the first one whereby they assume that the premium which has to be paid for the second order is smaller than the profit margin. If this is not the case, the second order should be zero. They solve this model with a distribution-free approach and thereby determine a lower bound on the expected profit. They conclude that when having a second order opportunity the size of the first order is smaller and the lower bound on the expected profit is larger than in the classical newsvendor model with a single order. Based on their work, Khouja (1996) presents an important review article about the newsvendor model with emergency supply. Two objective functions, namely maximizing the expected profit and maximizing the probability to achieve a target profit, are considered. In addition to that, it is assumed that a certain amount of demand which is not satisfied from the first order is lost because not all customers are willing to wait. In line with Gallego and Moon (1993) it is concluded that the first order quantity is reduced if a second order is possible and that dual sourcing can help to increase profitability. Also Eeckhoudt et al. (1995) consider the possibility of an emergency order during the selling season which can be received for additional cost.

Related to this, Lau and Lau (1998) present decision models for single-period products with two ordering opportunities. With their work they want to provide decision support for operations managers of newsvendor-type products on how much to order or produce initially, when to place the second order, if at all, and for which quantity. The planning period is split into two time slots whereby the orders arrive at the beginning of each time slot and demand in each time slot is normally distributed with known parameters. They also conclude that by having a second order opportunity the first order quantity is reduced. In addition they point out that the second order opportunity becomes more valuable if demand variability increases and it is more valuable for products with a low profit margin.

Also the concept of reactive capacity is related to dual sourcing. Reactive capacity in this respect means that in addition to make-to-stock production, which is similar to ordering before the selling season, additional make-to-order production is possible during the season to satisfy demand. The reactive capacity can be limited allowing only for a certain amount of additional production or unlimited which means that all demand can be fulfilled (Cachon and Terwiesch, 2009). Chung et al. (2008) present a multi-item newsvendor problem with unlimited, preseasonal production and reactive, capacitated production during the selling season. The reactive quantity is produced by internal capacity whereas the preseason order is outsourced to a supplier. Before the beginning of the selling season, for each item the order quantity which will be delivered by the external source is fixed and the reactive capacity is allocated to the different items. It is assumed that this allocation can not be altered during the season, even though the internal production during the season takes place under full knowledge of demand. With their model they provide decision support on how much to order preseasonally and how to allocate internal capacity; furthermore, the value of internal capacity and its contribution to a company's profit is evaluated. The classical multi-item newsvendor model and the expected profit function is extended by including the costs for the reactive production and a constraint for the internal capacity is defined. In contrast to the models with unlimited, reactive capacity, in this case lost sales can occur if the allocation of the internal capacity for a certain item is not sufficient. The bisection method is used to find the optimal solution to this problem. It is shown that the optimal order quantity derived by the classical newsvendor is an upper bound for the optimal preseasonal order quantity and a lower bound for the total order quantity, which is the sum of the preseasonal and the reactive quantity. As in the single-item case, increasing demand volatility increases the value of reactive capacity. If the demand volatility of a single item increases, then for that single item the amount allocated to reactive capacity increases, but for all the other items the preseasonal quantities increase and the reactive quantities decrease. This confirms the idea of Fisher (1997) about the alignment of product types and supply chain strategies; it is reasonable to shift the production for items with rather stable demand to the preseasonal stage and reserve reactive capacity for those items with higher demand variability.

Zhang and Du (2010) present a multi-product newsboy problem with limited capacity and outsourcing. In this case a certain amount of the products is produced internally whereas the company tries to satisfy any demand which can not be fulfilled from the internal supply by procuring goods from a third-party. Due to the multi-product assumption, in addition to balancing the cost of understocking with the additional cost of outsourcing, the in-house capacity has to be allocated to different products. The objective is to maximize expected profit by determining the optimal in-house and outsourcing quantities. The external supply source has no capacity limitation but there are two different outsourcing variants, one with zero lead time and one with non-zero lead time. With zero lead time outsourcing, all demand can be satisfied by the sum of in-house production and outsourcing and the outsourcing can be seen as emergency supply option or reactive, unlimited capacity, as described above. In the case of non-zero lead time outsourcing some demand might be lost or backordered. In this case, it has to be decided how much to produce internally and how much to outsource for each product before demand realization. In contrast to zero lead time outsourcing, where only the internal production has to be determined before demand is known, both decisions have to be made in one stage. They develop a solution algorithm for the non-zero lead time outsourcing and compare the results of the two variants. They conclude that the zero lead time outsourcing is preferable to the non-zero lead time variant, if the outsourcing costs are equal. But in general, the costs for "immediate" delivery will be higher so the choice for one or the other variant is not clear-cut.

The concept of quick response is also closely related to dual sourcing. The term quick response stems from the apparel industry and refers to the fact that the retailer has the ability to adjust his orders if better demand information becomes available (see, for instance, Fisher and Raman, 1996). Quick response is also related to lead time reductions and thereby allowing retailers to order closer to the start of the selling season or even to order more than once for a selling season (Chopra and Meindl, 2010). Also Iyer and Bergen (1997) analyse the value of quick response for manufacturers and retailers in the apparel industry and identify conditions under which quick response can lead to a win-win situation. Choi and Chow (2008) add to this field of research by showing how different strategies, such as buy-back contracts or service-level commitments, can help to achieve a win-win situation. Beside expected profit they also consider the risk involved, which is expressed by the variance of the profit.

The papers presented so far have shown that dual sourcing can help to increase expected profit, reduce costs and increase service level compared to single sourcing. But dual sourcing can also be a measure to mitigate supply chain (disruption) risks. Berger and Zeng (2006) present an approach for deciding on the optimal number of suppliers in the presence of risk based on the expected costs. Dada et al. (2007) analyse a newsvendor model with unreliable suppliers. The decision maker has to decide whether to place an order with an uncertain supplier and if yes, for which quantity. The unreliability relates to the fact that the quantity received is no more than and, in general, lower than the order quantity. They conclude that their model has the same structural properties as the newsvendor model with multiple and fully reliable suppliers and it helps to investigate the trade-off between cost and reliability. It turns out that cost and not reliability is the decisive factor for supplier selection which means that perfect reliability is no guarantee to be chosen as supplier.

In line with this, Yu et al. (2009) point out that dual sourcing can be an effective strategy to cope with unexpected supply break-downs. The company can rely on two suppliers with unlimited capacity. On the one hand, there is an offshore supplier, located outside the company's country which offers a low price and is the main supplier but may suffer from disruptions. On the other hand, the company can use a local supplier, which is more expensive but also more reliable. The offshore supplier breaks down completely with a certain probability in each supply cycle. They compare the expected profit functions of two single (pure offshore vs. pure local sourcing) with a dual sourcing strategy under supply disruptions and identify the factors which make the one or the other strategy preferable. The decisive factor is the disruption probability: If the disruption probability is smaller than a first threshold pure offshore sourcing should be chosen; if it is between the first and the second threshold dual sourcing is the best strategy with respect to expected profit; if it is greater than the second threshold pure local sourcing should be chosen.

Hou et al. (2010) consider dual sourcing with a backup supplier under supply risk and investigate coordination with a buy-back contract. They consider two types of risk, namely disruption risk which results in a complete non-delivery and recurrent risk which is reflected in an uncertain delivery volume. Li et al. (2010) also deal with the coordination and cooperation of a retailer with two suppliers under risk based on the newsvendor framework. The two suppliers are subject to failures which lead to the non-delivery of the order quantities. In the case of failure, the retailer is able to procure the missing items from the spot market, but for a higher cost than from the known suppliers. In this model, the spot market can be seen as backup supplier. In addition, it is assumed that the costs of the suppliers increase depending on their reliability, which is expressed by the probability of failure. A centralized system, in which all the decisions are taken in order to maximize the performance of the whole supply chain, is compared to the decentralized solution with two suppliers which either set the wholesale price individually or collectively. By this, the trade-off between reliability of suppliers and their related costs as well as the value of centralized decision-making in supply chains is analysed.

The basic model for our work is taken from Warburton and Stratton (2005) who analyse dual sourcing with onshore and offshore sourcing based on the newsvendor model. The assumptions are to a great extent in line with Gallego and Moon (1993) and Khouja (1996). They show in their work that dual sourcing is advantageous from an economic perspective, considering expected profit and the cycle service level. The first order is placed with the cheap, offshore supplier. The onshore supplier is then used to fulfil any demand which is not satisfied by the offshore supplier, thereby a cycle service level of 100% can be achieved. In addition to that, even though a premium has to be paid for the onshore supplier, this strategy increases the expected profit compared to a single offshore sourcing strategy. A dual sourcing strategy, in general, outperforms a single sourcing strategy; it is more valuable when the variability of demand is high and the premium which has to be paid is low. The same conclusions are drawn by Cachon and Terwiesch (2009) but in their work no specific assumptions about the geographical location of the two supply sources are made. They simply assume that there is a cheap, inflexible supply source and a flexible, more expensive supply source. But overall, they derive the same conclusions as Warburton and Stratton (2005).

The topic of dual and multiple suppliers is also investigated with the help of multi-period inventory models. An overview of multiple-supplier inventory models is provided by Minner (2003). Veeraraghavan and Scheller-Wolf (2008) present a simple policy for a periodically reviewed single-stage inventory system. Their work is extended by Yazlali and Erhun (2008) and Klosterhalfen et al. (2010) who analyse the value of two suppliers with complementary service in the multi-period case. Zhou and Chao (2010) analyse serial supply chains with regular and expedited shipping and derive upper and lower bounds for the optimal control parameters. Allon and van Mieghem (2010) develop a tailored base-surge policy for dual sourcing in the case of near- and offshore production. They show that it is reasonable to order the "base" demand at a constant rate from the offshore supplier in order to exploit the cost advantage of the offshore supplier and the "surge" demand which is the remaining volatile part is satisfied from the fast, nearshore source. They provide an upper bound for the quantity allocated to the offshore source which is always lower than the average demand. In general, the offshore order quantity decisively depends on the average demand. It is high when the cost advantage of the offshore source is high, holding cost and cost of capital are low and the difference in transportation time between the offshore and the nearshore source is rather small. However, a high demand uncertainty and a high supply uncertainty of the offshore source favours the use of the nearshore source. These results are in line with those derived from the single-period models.

4.3 Transport-focused dual sourcing framework

We develop a transport-focused dual sourcing framework with an offshore and an onshore supplier in order to point out the relation of dual sourcing and transport. In addition to that, the framework comprises the external conditions, i.e. environmental regulations for transport, which have an influence on the company's decision(s).

In the single-period dual sourcing model based on the newsvendor framework it is assumed that in addition to the order before the selling season a supplementary order during the selling season is possible. The company relies on a cheap but slow and inflexible supply source as well as on an expensive but fast and flexible supply source. According to Warburton and Stratton (2005), we assume that the first supply source is located in a low-cost country, like China, which is far away from the market and has a long lead time. This supply source is called the offshore supplier. The second supply source is located close to the market and is denoted as the onshore supplier. Furthermore, this source can react immediately to changes in demand and it is assumed to have unlimited capacity. The onshore supplier is used as backup supplier in order to fulfil any demand which can not be satisfied by the offshore supplier. The onshore supplier can also be a production facility owned by the company which carries out flexible make-to-order production. This is possible as, in general, the quantity ordered from the offshore supplier is larger than the quantity ordered from the onshore supplier in order to exploit the cost advantage. Furthermore, for reasonable assumptions of the cost and price parameters the offshore order quantity is generally smaller than the expected demand (Warburton and Stratton, 2005, Cachon and Terwiesch, 2009).

Due to the fact that the first supplier is located in an offshore country a long transport distance must be overcome in order to bring the products to the market. This long transport distance results in high transport activity and high carbon emissions from transport. The transport from offshore locations, in general, is carried out by sea or by air whereby the latter is considered as being much more environmentally unfriendly. In contrast to this, it is assumed that there is (nearly) no transport needed to deliver the products from the onshore supplier to the market.

In order to illustrate the different environmental impact of transport from the two suppliers we exemplarily compare the CO_2e emissions with the help of a carbon emission calculation tool for transport called EcoTransIT. The transport from Beijing (China) to Vienna (Austria) via ocean shipping as main transport mode is compared to the transport from Bratislava (Slovakia) to Vienna (Austria) by truck. The calculation is done for one ton of an average good as defined in the calculation tool. The transport from the offshore source results in CO_2e emissions of 129 kg; the transport from the onshore source produces considerably lower emissions and results in only 5.8 kg CO_2e. This clearly shows the negative environmental impact of offshore sourcing if only carbon emissions from transport are considered. The difference is even greater when air transport is used instead of ocean shipping. Then, the air transport from the offshore location would result in 5444 kg CO_2e for one ton of the transported goods (EcoTransIT, 2010).

The negative impact of offshoring and offshore sourcing on transport carbon emissions is also pointed out by Cadarso et al. (2010). It is evident that offshore sourcing results in an increase of transport carbon emissions. But it has to be kept in mind that for some products the total carbon emissions, consisting of emissions from transport and manufacturing, might be lower if the offshore source can produce the products in a way which result in low manufacturing emissions and the difference outweighs the increase of transport carbon emissions. For instance, for fresh food produce (vegetables, fruits, etc.) which is purchased off-season in Europe it is more environmentally friendly to import it from offshore locations than to produce it locally. This is due to the fact that, off-season, these products can be grown without requiring much energy in the offshore location. So the lower (indirect) carbon emissions from the offshore production outweigh the increase of transport carbon emissions (Smith et al., 2005). This picture, of course, looks different, for other products, such as consumer electronics, where climate conditions do not have an influence on the manufacturing process and the energy needed. For these products, it has to be kept in mind that energy production, in general, is much more environmentally unfriendly in typical offshore countries, such as China (IEA, 2009). Considering that, from an environmental point of view, the offshore source would lose its attractiveness due to high carbon emissions from transport and manufacturing.

In our framework, we do not explicitly consider the production processes of the offshore and onshore supplier and thereby assume that the same amount of emissions stems from the production processes. Even though this is a limiting assumption, it allows us to solely investigate the impact of the sourcing strategy on the transport carbon emissions within the supply chain.

Table 4.3 gives an overview of the transport-focused dual sourcing framework. External conditions, which are in our case environmental regulations for transport, impose restrictions on companies and therefore influence the policies they choose. Three possible environmental regulations are examined in more detail in our work. Firstly, a strict limit for transport carbon emissions is considered which is a constraint for the company's offshore ordering decision. Secondly, a linear transport emission tax is imposed on each unit ordered from the offshore supplier. And thirdly, it is assumed that an emission trading

Table 4.3: Transport-focused dual sourcing framework

External conditions	Environmental regulations for transport
	Emission limit *or*
	Linear emission taxes *or*
	Emission trading
Policy	Dual sourcing
	with off- and onshore supply source
Decision(s)	Offshore order quantity
	which determines transport carbon emissions

scheme is valid for the transport sector. The company has to decide before the selling season how much to order from the offshore supplier and the offshore order quantity is directly related to the transport carbon emissions. Therefore, the offshore ordering decision is influenced by the environmental regulations; it determines if the emission limit is met, what amount of emission tax has to be paid or how many emission allowances are needed.

It is important to relate the emission limit, i.e. the number of allowances allocated to a certain company, and the emission taxes to product units to be able to model the different environmental regulations. Hoen et al. (2010) include the environmental aspect into the transport mode choice and they present in a very detailed way how to derive emission factors of different transport modes and how to allocate the emission factors of a vehicle to one product unit which is transported. By analogy with their idea we assume that the policy instruments are broken down to company level and related to one unit of the product.

As described in Section 2.4 and in accordance with Hoen et al. (2010) the transport carbon emissions mainly depend on the parameters transport mode and vehicle type used, distance travelled, load factor and type of product (volume and weight). The distance travelled and the transport mode are determined by the location of the offshore supplier. Assuming that the transport is carried out by a logistics service provider average values can be taken for the other parameters and an average transport carbon emission factor (CO_2e tons per product unit) can be derived. With the help of this average transport carbon emission factor per product unit the environmental regulations can be integrated in the decision-making of the company.

The emission tax can be implemented in two different ways, either as a constant value "penalizing" offshore sourcing not considering the carbon emissions caused by the transport activity or depending on the (calculated or estimated) emissions produced by the transport activity. In the latter case, based on the average transport carbon emission factor (CO_2e tons per product unit) the carbon emission tax for one product unit is derived by multiplying the carbon emission tax for one ton of CO_2e with the average transport carbon emission factor. This average transport carbon emission factor is also necessary for operationalising an emission limit and an emission trading scheme. In general, emission allowances certify the right to emit one ton of CO_2e. Therefore, in order to be able to directly relate order quantity and emission limit to each other the emission limit has to be translated into product units. For more details on how to derive a transport carbon emission factor for one product unit and how to relate policy instruments to a product unit the reader is referred to Hoen et al. (2010).

4.4 Single-period dual sourcing model

In the following we present the basic dual sourcing model based on the newsvendor framework and extend it by including a strict emission limit, linear emission taxes and emission trading for the transport from the offshore supplier to the market. We compare the different models based on the economic performance measured by the expected profit. Furthermore, the environmental performance of the company is considered whereby the offshore order quantity serves as an indicator for transport carbon emissions. We also compare the results to a single offshore strategy, i.e. the classical newsvendor model with a single ordering possibility (see Section 4.1). The notation for the basic dual sourcing model and its extensions is summarized in Table 4.4.

4.4.1 Basic dual sourcing model

In the basic single-period dual sourcing model with an offshore and an onshore supplier it is assumed that the offshore order quantity q has to be placed when demand is still random. Because of the long procurement lead time for delivering the products from the offshore supplier products from this source can be ordered only once during the selling season. But additional units of the product can be procured from the onshore supplier in the case not enough units of the product have been ordered from the offshore supplier. Note that the decision of how much to order from the offshore supplier has to be taken under demand uncertainty while the products from the onshore supplier are procured after demand has been realized which means that this decision is taken under certainty. The product is sold to the market for the selling price per unit p. On the procurement side, the purchase price per unit differs between the two sources. The purchase price per unit from the offshore supplier is the product price per unit c; the purchase price per unit from the onshore supplier is obtained by adding a domestic premium per unit d to the product price per

Table 4.4: Notation for the basic dual sourcing model and its extensions

p	selling price per unit
c	product price per unit/purchase price per unit from the offshore supplier
d	domestic premium per unit
z	salvage value per unit
q	offshore order quantity
x	realized demand
X	random demand
F	demand distribution function
F^{-1}	inverse of demand distribution function
q^*	optimal offshore order quantity with dual sourcing
q^{on}	expected onshore order quantity
$P(q, x)$	random profit depending on offshore order quantity q and realized demand x
$P(q)$	expected profit depending on offshore order quantity q
t	emission tax per unit ordered from offshore
b	buying price of emission allowance for one product unit
s	selling price of emission allowance for one product unit
L	emission limit expressed in product units
$P_t(q)$	expected profit including emission tax t
$P_b(q)$	expected profit including costs of buying emission allowances
$P_s(q)$	expected profit including revenue of selling emission allowances
$P_L(q)$	expected profit with emission trading
q^{limit}	optimal offshore order quantity with emission limit L
q^t	optimal offshore order quantity with emission tax t
q^b	argmax $P_b(q)$
q^s	argmax $P_s(q)$
q^L	optimal offshore order quantity with emission trading
$E()$	expected value
$(x)^+$	$\max(x, 0)$

unit c. This premium is mainly due to higher labour costs that have to be paid in the onshore production facility and also reflects the flexibility provided by the onshore supplier. Usually, the regular transport costs are negligible in relation to the total costs, so they are not considered. Any leftover inventory can be sold at the end of the season for a salvage value per unit z. We assume $p > c > z$ and $p > (c + d) > z$. An overview of the different stages in the supply chain is given in Figure 4.1.

Then the profit P depends on the offshore order quantity q and on the realized demand x:

$$P(q, x) = \begin{cases} p \cdot x - c \cdot q + z \cdot (q - x) & x \leq q \\ p \cdot x - c \cdot q - (c + d) \cdot (x - q) & x > q \end{cases} \tag{4.5}$$

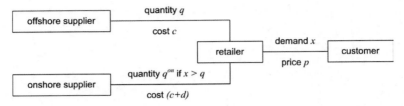

Figure 4.1: Dual sourcing with off- and onshore supplier

For $x \leq q$ only the offshore source is used to fulfil all demand and any leftover inventory can be salvaged for the value z. For $x > q$ additional units are procured from the onshore source in order to fulfil all demand. The expected profit depending on the offshore order quantity q is given by:

$$P(q) = E(p \cdot X + z(q - X)^+ - c \cdot q - (c + d)(X - q)^+) \qquad (4.6)$$

whereby $E()$ represents the expected value and $(x)^+$ is $\max(x, 0)$. So, the expected profit consists of the revenue generated by the selling of the products for p per unit during the season and for z per unit after the season less the cost for ordering from the offshore for c per unit and the onshore supplier for $(c + d)$ per unit.

By maximizing the expected profit, the optimal offshore order quantity for the risk-neutral decision maker can be derived and is given by (see, for instance Warburton and Stratton, 2005, Cachon and Terwiesch, 2009):

$$q^* = F^{-1} \left(\frac{d}{d + c - z} \right) \qquad (4.7)$$

Again, the expression in the brackets is the well-known critical fractile or critical ratio which represents the probability that the realized demand is lower or equal than the order quantity, i.e. cycle service level. The offshore order quantity is either used to satisfy demand or results in leftover inventory which can then be sold for a salvage value. So, the cost of overstocking per unit is $(c - z)$ which is the same as in the model with a single order opportunity. In contrast to the classical model where lost sales are possible and the contribution margin $(p - c)$ is considered as the cost of understocking per unit, in the dual sourcing model the cost of understocking equals to the domestic premium d. Thanks to the onshore supplier who serves as backup all demand can be satisfied and therefore no contribution margin is lost. However, a premium has to be paid for that. As long as the domestic premium d is smaller than the contribution margin per unit $(p-c)$ the onshore supplier is used to some extent. Of course, a higher domestic premium reduces the use of the onshore supplier, and vice versa. If $d > (p - c)$ demand should exclusively be satisfied from the offshore supplier. Generally, the offshore order quantity is smaller than in the model with a single order opportunity (see, for instance, Gallego and Moon, 1993, Khouja, 1996), which is in our case single offshore sourcing. Furthermore, for normally distributed demand the optimal offshore order quantity is smaller than the mean demand when the critical fractile is < 0.5. Taking (4.7) and assuming $z = 0$, this is the case when $d < c$.

The onshore order quantity, then, is used to fulfil any demand that can not be satisfied by the offshore order quantity. The expected onshore order quantity q^{on} equals to the expected lost sales in the newsvendor model, i.e. the expected number of units which exceeds the offshore order quantity. The expected onshore order quantity q^{on} is given by:

$$q^{on} = E((X - q)^+) \qquad (4.8)$$

It has to be kept in mind that the onshore supplier is only used, if demand is larger than the offshore order quantity, so no leftover inventory results from the onshore order quantity.

As already described in Section 4.2.2, the dual sourcing strategy outperforms a single offshore sourcing strategy with respect to expected profit. In various works it is shown that relying on two supply sources helps to reduce the expected mismatch costs which directly leads to an increase of expected profit. Furthermore, with the help of dual sourcing a higher service level can be achieved. It is intuitive that the offshore order quantity as well as the increase in profitability highly depends on the domestic premium and the demand uncertainty. A higher domestic premium leads to a higher offshore order quantity as the cost advantage outweighs the uncertainty under which the decision has to be taken, i.e. the total expected cost of overstocking. On the other hand, the higher the demand uncertainty the more a retailer is willing to rely on the onshore supplier thereby reducing the risk of overstocking (see, for instance, Warburton and Stratton, 2005, Cachon and Terwiesch, 2009).

With respect to environmental performance, it can be seen by comparing (4.4) and (4.7) that the (offshore) order quantity with a single order possibility is larger than the offshore order quantity with a dual sourcing strategy, i.e. $q_{cl}^* \geq q^*$. As the order quantity is directly related to the transport carbon emissions it can be concluded that by using dual sourcing strategy instead of single offshore sourcing the transport carbon emissions can be reduced while improving the economic performance. The actual improvements of the economic and environmental performance of the company depends on the cost and price parameters as well as the demand distribution.

4.4.2 Dual sourcing with transport emission limit

In a first step the model is extended by including a fixed limit L for transport carbon emissions. This means that the company receives a certain number of emission allowances free of charge. The emission allowances are then used to cover the emissions produced by the transport for bringing the products from the offshore supplier to the market. The company is not allowed to exceed this limit and therefore the emission limit L represents a constraint on the company's decision. To include the limit in the decision of the company the emission limit has to be expressed in product units, i.e. an emission allowance is used to cover the carbon emissions produced by the transport of one unit from the offshore supplier. The idea of a strict emission limit for offshore sourcing can be related to imposing import quotas for products procured from offshore suppliers.

By assuming this kind of regulation, the offshore order quantity is as follows:

$$
q^{limit} = \min\left(q^*, L\right) = \min\left(F^{-1}\left(\frac{d}{d + c - z}\right), L \right) \tag{4.9}
$$

If the optimal offshore order quantity q^* is smaller than the emission limit L the expected profit $P(q^*)$ can be generated. If the optimal order quantity q^* is larger than the emission limit L only the profit $P(L)$ is realized which is the profit resulting from ordering a quantity from the offshore supplier which corresponds exactly to the emission limit L. So, if the emission limit L is low the company can not order the profit-maximizing offshore order quantity which can strongly reduce the profitability of the company. However, the environmental performance of the company is improved. For instance, with an emission limit $L = 0$ all units are procured from the onshore source and the offshore source is not used at all. Due to the assumption that no transport carbon emissions are produced when ordering from the onshore supplier, the transport carbon emissions are even reduced to zero. With increasing emission limit L the offshore order quantity is increased until the optimal order quantity q^* is reached. In that case, the company yields the maximal expected profit and has no incentive to alter its decision. Then, if $L > q^*$, an amount of $(q^* - L)$ allowances remains unused. Due to a missing market for emission allowances no revenue can be generated from the selling of the excessive allowances.

For policy-making, a strict limit on transport carbon emissions seems to be an effective measure as the transport carbon emissions can be strongly reduced. But it has to be kept in mind that the economic performance of the company is reduced drastically for small L. In addition to that, a measure which imposes tight restrictions on the decision-making of individual companies is very difficult to implement.

In order to be restrictive the emission limit L has to be lower than the expected demand because for reasonable assumptions of the cost and price parameters the offshore order quantity is smaller than the expected demand (Warburton and Stratton, 2005, Cachon and Terwiesch, 2009). Furthermore, the offshore order quantity depends on the variability of demand and the cost advantage of the offshore source represented by the domestic premium d. So, in addition to detailed demand information, policy-makers would also need information about the further parameters which companies consider in their sourcing decision in order to set a restricting emission limit. Furthermore, policy-making would have to evaluate the impact of their restriction on the economic performance of individual companies.

4.4.3 Dual sourcing model with linear transport emission tax

In a second step, the basic model is extended by including emission costs for the transport from the offshore source. We assume a linear transport emission tax on each unit ordered from the offshore supplier. This idea is related to an import tax based on the carbon content of products as proposed by Huebler (2009). A similar model including transport emission cost can be found in Rosič et al. (2009).

Similar to the first model extension, it is assumed that no transport emission are produced when ordering from the onshore supplier. The transport carbon emission tax per unit is denoted by t and we assume that it is a a linear tax. The transport emission tax is given as monetary unit per ton of CO_2e which is fixed by policy-making. The emission tax for a product unit then depends on the carbon emission produced by the transport of a product unit. An average transport carbon emission factor can be assumed if the transport is carried out by a logistics service provider which usually achieves high vehicle utilization irrespective of the transport quantity of a single customer. So, the logistics service provider can determine the average amount of carbon emissions produced by the transport of a product unit which then is used to calculate the transport carbon emission tax t per product unit.

The offshore supplier is only used if it is overall cheaper than the onshore supplier which is the case as long as $t < d$. As soon as $t \geq d$ the product is exclusively procured from the onshore supplier on demand. The additional cost for the offshore supplier has to be considered in decision-making and in the expected profit function. Considering a linear emission tax t, the expected profit is given by:

$$P_t(q) = E(p \cdot X + z(q - X)^+ - (c + t) \cdot q - (c + d)(X - q)^+) \qquad (4.10)$$

Then the optimal offshore order quantity, i.e. the profit-maximizing order quantity, is:

$$q^t = F^{-1}\left(\frac{d - t}{d + c - z}\right) \qquad (4.11)$$

The offshore order quantity q^t depends on the relative cost advantage that can be achieved through offshore sourcing. With increasing emission tax t the company sources less from offshore because the cost advantage is reduced. The total order quantity (off- and onshore quantity) also decreases as t increases. This is due to the following relation:

$$q^t + q^{on} = E(X) + E((q - X)^+) \qquad (4.12)$$

The left hand side of the equation is the expected total order quantity, which is the sum of the offshore order quantity q^t and the expected onshore order quantity q^{on}. The total order quantity is either used to fulfil demand or results in leftover inventory. Due to the fact that the decision how much to order from the onshore supplier is taken under demand certainty no leftovers result from that decision. Leftover inventory only results from the offshore ordering decision. So with increasing t the offshore order quantity and the expected leftover inventory $(E((q - X)^+))$ decrease and overall, the total order quantity converges to the expected demand $(E(X))$.

Comparing (4.7) and (4.11) it is evident that the offshore order quantity with an emission tax $t > 0$ is smaller than the offshore order quantity in the basic dual sourcing model, i.e. $q^t < q^*$. Due to this fact, also the transport activity from the offshore supplier and the related carbon emissions are reduced. This helps to improve the environmental performance of the company. The actual improvement potential decisively depends on the values of the different parameters. But due to the additional costs as a negative side effect the expected profit is reduced as well and therefore the economic performance is harmed.

As already stated, the emission tax reduces the cost advantage of the offshore supplier and induces the retailer to rely to a larger extent on the onshore supplier. So for policy-making, it can be concluded that also with the help of a linear transport emission tax the amount sourced from the offshore supplier and together with that transport carbon emissions can be reduced. But in contrast to imposing a strict emission limit, where it is clear that a certain emission reduction is achieved, it is not clear which amount of carbon emission reduction can be reached by a certain emission tax. This is also pointed out by Hoel (1998) as one of the disadvantages of environmental taxes. The emission reduction decisively depends on the demand and cost structure of the company. In particular the relation between the domestic premium d and the emission tax t influences the reduction potential. This issue is further investigated in Section 4.5 with the help of numerical analyses.

An advantage of an emission tax is that it considers the different cost structures of companies and allows those which achieve a high cost advantage from offshore sourcing to still exploit this advantage to some extent even after the introduction of the transport emission tax. Nevertheless, it can be expected that an additional tax is difficult to implement from policy perspective and resistance from industry could arise.

4.4.4 Dual sourcing model with emission trading for transport

In a third step, we include emission trading for transport in the basic model. Under the existing EU emission trading scheme (ETS) companies receive a certain number of allowances free of charge which are then used to cover the carbon emission produced by the installations. Additional emission allowances have to be bought if more emissions are produced than covered by the allowances or remaining, unused emission allowances can be sold. If an emission trading scheme is valid for transport activity then, in contrast to the previous model, transport emission costs would not arise for each unit ordered from the offshore supplier, but only if a certain threshold, i.e. the emission limit, is exceeded.

The mechanism of the EU ETS is not directly applicable to emission trading for transport. First of all, an emission trading scheme for transport would have to be implemented on a global scale in order to be effective (Sinn, 2009). And in the transport sector, the allocation of emission allowances would pose a much higher challenge due to the significant higher number of participants (Raux, 2004).

There are two possible variants of an emission trading scheme for transport. In the first variant, the emission allowances for transport are allocated to logistics service providers for the pollution which is produced by the transport activity. The logistics service providers further allocate the received allowances to their customers based on the contractual agreements (see Raux, 2010, for the conceptual idea). It is agreed between the two parties that the company can also demand more transport capacity than possible with the company's allocated emission limit but has to pay the emission buying price b for the excessive use. On the other hand, if the company uses less than the allocated emission limit the remaining allowances can be given back to the logistics service provider for a premium, i.e. the emission selling price s, which can then use the returned allowances for providing transport services to other customers. In this case, policy-making has only limited influence on the company's ordering decision; policy-makers can only control the amount of carbon emissions produced by logistics service providers and do not have an impact on the company which is actually responsible for the produced transport carbon emissions.

In contrast to this, the emission allowances could also be allocated to the company which orders the products. Then, the company which wants the transport to be carried out by a third-party has to provide the necessary emission allowances to the logistics service provider. The emission allowances would certify the right to emit an amount of emissions which is produced by shipping one product unit from the offshore supplier to the market. When the offshore order quantity q exceeds the emission limit L, which is expressed in units of the product, the company has to acquire extra emission allowances for the emission buying price per unit b. In the opposite case, when $q < L$ the company is able to sell the remaining unused emission allowances for the emission selling price per unit s to other companies needing more emission allowances than they have received from the authorities. Letmathe and Balakrishnan (2005) state that due to differences in transaction costs the buying price is typically higher than the selling price of emission allowances. According to that it is assumed that $b \geq s$. With this system, policy-making could (rather) directly influence the offshore ordering decisions of companies. Such a system can be related to regulations such as (free) import quotas together with import taxes based on the carbon content of a product.

We consider the second variant of an emission trading scheme for transport. In order to be able to model it we have to abstract from the real-world system and simplify it. Therefore, it has to be kept in mind that the results are also not directly transferable to a real-world setting but only give an indication on how a similar system could impact the decision(s) of individual companies. Firstly, as already stated, we assume that the emission limit L is expressed in units of the product and an allowance covers the emissions produced by the transport of one product unit from the offshore supplier to the market. Secondly, we assume that the prices for emission allowances are exogenously fixed. Actually, they are determined by the market and depend on the scarcity of emission allowances which is mainly determined by the overall emission limit imposed by the authorities. Therefore, the prices of emission allowances could be modelled as a decreasing function of the emission limit, as mentioned by Hua et al. (2011), but this is beyond the scope of our work. Thirdly, we assume that the company's number of emission allowances to be sold/bought is rather small compared to the whole market volume for emission allowances. So the company can buy and sell any quantity of emission allowances.

Considering the second variant of emission trading where emission allowances are allocated to the company making the ordering decision the expected profit is derived as follows. The expected profit of the company is composed of the base profit $P(q)$ given by (4.6) which is the expected profit of the dual sourcing model without environmental regulations. Depending on the relation between q and L, revenue for the selling of emission allowances is added or the cost for buying additional emission allowances is deducted. The expected profit for an emission limit $L > 0$ and offshore order quantity q is then defined as follows:

$$P_L(q) = \begin{cases} P_s(q) \text{ for } q \leq L \\ P_b(q) \text{ for } q > L \end{cases} \tag{4.13}$$

with

$$P_s(q) = P(q) + s(L - q) \tag{4.14}$$
$$P_b(q) = P(q) - b(q - L) \tag{4.15}$$

As long as the order quantity q is below or equal to the emission limit L the profit $P_s(q)$ is generated which consists of the base profit and the revenue generated through the selling of unused emission allowances. In this case, s represents an opportunity cost; if a unit is procured from the offshore supplier, the emission allowance for that unit has to be used and this emission allowance can no longer be sold, therefore the company forgoes potential revenue. When more units are ordered than covered by the allocated emission allowances, additional allowances have to be bought which reduces the base profit to $P_b(q)$. The emission buying price b is an actual cost which incurs for each unit ordered which exceeds the emission limit L.

It is well known that $P(q)$ is a concave function (see, for instance, Khouja, 1996, 1999). Obviously, this property carries over to $P_s(q)$ and $P_b(q)$. Because of $b \geq s$ the following inequalities hold:

$$P_s(q) \leq P_b(q) \text{ for } q \leq L \tag{4.16}$$
$$P_s(q) > P_b(q) \text{ for } q > L \tag{4.17}$$

Therefore, according to (4.13), the expected profit $P_L(q)$ can be written in the following way:

$$P_L(q) = \min\left(P_s(q), P_b(q)\right) \tag{4.18}$$

Consequently, $P_L(q)$ is a concave function because the minimum of concave functions is again concave (see, e.g., Rockafellar, 1997, Theorem 5.5.).

To derive the optimal offshore order quantity q^L, we define $q^b = \text{argmax } P_b(q)$ and $q^s = \text{argmax } P_s(q)$ with:

$$q^b = F^{-1}\left(\frac{d-b}{d+c-z}\right) \tag{4.19}$$

and

$$q^s = F^{-1}\left(\frac{d-s}{d+c-z}\right) \tag{4.20}$$

Note that q^b and q^s are derived like the optimal order quantity in the classical newsvendor model.

Due to the fact that the selling price s is smaller than or equal to the buying price b the optimal order quantity q^s is always larger than or equal to q^b, i.e. $q^s \geq q^b$. Note that q^b and q^s do not depend on the emission limit L. Therefore, q^L can be characterized in dependence of L.

If $L < q^b \leq q^s$, then according to (4.17) $q^L = q^b$. Complementary, if $L > q^s \geq q^b$, then $q^L = q^s$ because of (4.16). Finally, if $q^b \leq L \leq q^s$, P_L attains its maximum for $q^L = L$ because:

$$P(L) = P_b(L) = P_s(L) \tag{4.21}$$

This is also illustrated in Figure 4.7.

Summarizing, for an emission limit $L > 0$ the optimal offshore order quantity q^L is a two-sided control limit policy given by:

$$q^L = \begin{cases} q^b & \text{for } L < q^b \\ L & \text{for } q^b \leq L \leq q^s \\ q^s & \text{for } L > q^s \end{cases} \qquad (4.22)$$

Thus, the optimal offshore order quantity q^L given by (4.22) crucially depends on the relation between the lower control limit q^b, the upper control limit q^s and the emission limit L. For $L < q^b \leq q^s$, it is better for the enterprise to buy some extra allowances than to rely to a larger extent on the onshore supplier. For $L > q^s \geq q^b$, it is better to generate revenue through the selling of allowances and rely to a larger extent on the onshore supplier than sourcing more units from the offshore supplier and risking leftover inventory. For $q^b \leq L \leq q^s$, it is not reasonable for the company to either sell or buy emission allowances.

The difference between the upper and the lower control limit depends on the values of the emission buying and selling price. If there is no difference between the buying and selling price of emission allowances, i.e. $b = s$, the impact of emission trading on the company's ordering decision is similar to a transport emission tax as concluded in, for instance, Benjaafar et al. (2010). If $b = s$, the company orders $q^L = q^b = q^s$ which is independent of the emission limit L. But it has to be kept in mind that the level of the emission limit has a decisive impact on the economic performance of the company.

The models presented in Sections 4.4.1, 4.4.2 and 4.4.3 are special cases of the extended model including emission trading. The basic dual sourcing model without consideration of environmental aspects is represented by the extended model with $s = 0$ and $b = 0$. The dual sourcing model with a strict emission limit can be modelled with a respective value for the emission limit L and $b = \infty$ and $s = 0$. The dual sourcing model with a linear transport emission tax corresponds to the extended model with $L = 0$ and $t = b$.

From the optimal ordering policy (4.22) we immediately see that irrespective of L, b and s the offshore order quantity with emission trading q^L is smaller than the offshore order quantity q^* given by (4.7). On the one hand, for any emission limit L the offshore order quantity is not larger than q^s, i.e. q^s is the maximal offshore order quantity. An emission limit $L > q^s \geq q^b$ allows the company to generate additional revenue without having to improve its environmental performance. On the other hand, for any emission limit L the offshore order quantity is not smaller than q^b, i.e. q^b is the minimal offshore order quantity. An emission limit $L < q^b \leq q^s$ would not help to reduce transport carbon emissions but would only hurt the economic performance and competitiveness of the company. For environmental policy-making it is, thus, reasonable to set the emission limit L to the minimal offshore order quantity, i.e. $L = q^b$. Specifying $L > q^b$, the transport carbon emissions are higher whereas $L < q^b$ leads to lower expected profit for the company because $P_L(q)$ is increasing in the emission limit L. These effects are further explored in the following section with the help of numerical analyses.

4.5 Numerical analyses

In order to gain more insights into the basic single-period dual sourcing model and its extensions with environmental regulations we perform numerical analyses. The basic cost and price parameters are listed in Table 4.5. Additional parameters are introduced when needed in the respective sections.

Table 4.5: Numerical analyses: Basic cost and price parameters

Selling price per unit p	20
Product price per unit c	10
Salvage value per unit z	5
Domestic premium per unit d	2

Demand is assumed to be normally distributed with the parameters summarized in Table 4.6. Different values for the standard deviation are taken in order to show the effect of increased demand variability. The demand distribution with σ_1 which is a very low value should be considered as extreme scenario. This helps to underline that in the case of low demand variability the value of dual sourcing is limited; this holds true for the basic model as well as its extensions.

Table 4.6: Numerical analyses: Demand scenarios

Mean demand μ	1000
Standard deviation σ_1	50
Standard deviation σ_2	150
Standard deviation σ_3	250

We compute and compare the results for the basic dual sourcing model and its extensions based on the formulas in Section 4.4 and perform sensitivity analyses in order to derive further implications for management and policy-making. For the single offshore sourcing model which also serves as reference point we apply the classical newsvendor model presented in Section 4.1. The calculations are done with the help of MS Excel and the necessary functions for the spreadsheet calculations can be found in Chopra and Meindl (2010, pp. 349).

4.5.1 Basic dual sourcing model

The results for the basic dual sourcing model in comparison to single offshore sourcing are summarized in Table 4.7. The results serve as reference point for the extensions of the dual sourcing model with environmental regulations.

Table 4.7: Comparison of single offshore sourcing and basic dual sourcing

	σ_1	σ_2	σ_3
Offshore order q with single offshoring	1022	1065	1108
Offshore order q with dual sourcing	972	915	859
Difference in %	-4.9	-14.1	-22.5
Expected profit with single offshoring	9727	9182	8637
Expected profit with dual sourcing	9881	9643	9405
Difference in %	$+1.6$	$+5.0$	$+8.9$

It can be seen that by switching from single offshore sourcing to dual sourcing the quantity ordered from the offshore supplier is reduced because the retailer to some extent relies on the onshore supplier for fulfilling demand. With dual sourcing, the expected onshore order quantities for the three demand scenarios are 37, 112 and 186, respectively. It is evident that a higher demand variability induces the retailer to rely more on the onshore supplier. The total order quantity with dual sourcing, i.e. the sum of offshore and onshore order quantity, is lower than the order quantity with a single offshore sourcing strategy. The expected profit is higher with dual sourcing than with single offshore sourcing, whereby the value of dual sourcing increases with demand variability. The profit increase ranges from 1.6% to 8.9%. By comparing the results for the two strategies, it can be seen that simply by using dual sourcing instead of single offshore sourcing the offshore order quantity is reduced and thereby a positive result for the environment is achieved without imposing any environmental regulations. The order quantity and thereby transport activity and related carbon emission can be reduced by 4.9% to 22.5% depending on the demand distribution.

A higher domestic premium d reduces the advantages of the onshore supplier with respect to flexibility and responsiveness. So with higher d the offshore order quantity increases until it reaches the value of the single offshore solution.

The expected profit, of course, decreases with increasing d until it equals the expected profit of the single offshore sourcing model. For $d > (p - c)$, the expected profit with dual sourcing is lower than the expected profit with single (offshore) sourcing, so the company should solely procure from the cheap, offshore source and the onshore supplier is not used at all. The results for the offshore order quantity and the expected profit for d varying between 2 and 10 are displayed in Figure 4.2. The curves showing the offshore order quantity intersect when the cost of understocking are equal to the cost of overstocking, i.e. $d = (c - z)$. In that case, the retailer orders exactly the mean demand and a cycle service level of 50% is achieved with $q^* = \mu$, irrespective of the demand variability, due to the assumption of normally distributed demand.

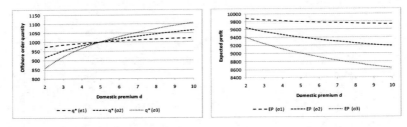

Figure 4.2: Basic dual sourcing: Offshore order quantity (left) and expected profit (right) depending on d

For policy-making it is important to note that a low domestic premium encourages companies to procure the products locally. This would help to improve the economic as well as the environmental performance. In this respect, the reduction of labour costs could help to reduce the domestic premium or subsidies granted to local suppliers would make them more cost-competitive. However it remains to be seen how these measures could be reasonably implemented.

4.5.2 Dual sourcing model with transport emission limit

The results for the dual sourcing model with a strict limit on carbon emissions from transport are presented in the following pargraphs. With an emission limit $L = 0$ a single onshore strategy is pursued which leads to a reduction of the expected profit to 8000 in any case, irrespective of the demand variability. This is due to the fact that all demand is satisfied from the flexible, onshore supplier. This decision is taken under complete certainty and in expectation exactly the mean demand μ is ordered.

For $L = 0$, the offshore order quantity is reduced to zero. This shows that a strict limit on carbon emissions from transport helps to reduce the carbon emissions. Under our simplifying assumption that no carbon emission result from onshore ordering, the carbon emissions are even reduced to zero. But it is also clearly shown that the economic performance of the company suffers. If the company is "forced" by an emission limit $L = 0$ to satisfy all demand from the onshore supplier the expected profit is reduced by 19.04%, 17.04% or 14.94% for σ_1, σ_2 and σ_3, respectively. It is clearly shown that expected profit of companies which order products with a low demand variability is more strongly reduced by the introduction of a strict emission limit. It is straightforward that the offshore order quantity increases linearly with increasing emission limit L until the optimal order quantity is reached. As soon as $L \geq q^*$, there is no need for the company to alter its decision. The results for the offshore order quantity and the expected profit for L varying between 0 and 1100 are shown in Figure 4.3.

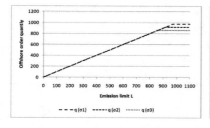 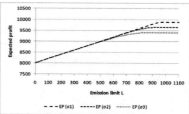

Figure 4.3: Dual sourcing with emission limit: Offshore order quantity (left) and expected profit (right) depending on L

The curve showing the expected profit runs nearly linearly in the case of a low emission limit. By allowing the retailer to order one more unit from the offshore supplier – starting from a very low level – the expected profit is simply increased by the domestic premium; the expected cost of overstocking which results from the increased offshore order quantity is negligibly small. This is no longer the case when the retailer already orders a significant amount from the offshore supplier. Then an additional unit procured from the offshore supplier helps to reduce cost by avoiding the domestic premium but at the same time the expected cost of overstocking increases. As soon as the retailer can procure the optimal offshore order quantity q^* the expected profit curve levels off and runs horizontally because the retailer has no incentive to change its decision. Due to a missing market, no revenue can be generated by selling remaining emission allowances.

For policy-making it can be concluded that a strict limit on carbon emissions from transport can be an effective measure to reduce the negative environmental impact from transport. However, if it is set to a low level it has a strong negative impact on the economic performance of individual companies.

4.5.3 Dual sourcing model with linear transport emission tax

In order to derive the numerical results for the dual sourcing model with a linear transport emission tax, we include an emission tax $t = 1.5$. It is intuitive that by introducing an emission tax the cost advantage of the offshore supplier is reduced and therefore, the offshore order quantity and the related transport activity are reduced. Furthermore, the expected profit is lower than in the basic dual sourcing model without a transport emission tax due to the additional costs. The numerical results for the model with a linear emission tax in comparison to the basic dual sourcing model are shown in Table 4.8.

Table 4.8: Comparison of basic dual sourcing and dual sourcing with emission tax $t = 1.5$

	σ_1	σ_2	σ_3
Offshore order q – basic DS	972	915	859
Offshore order q – DS with emission tax	927	780	634
Difference in %	−4.6	−14.8	−26.2
Expected profit – basic DS	9881	9643	9405
Expected profit – DS with emission tax	8452	8357	8261
Difference in %	−14.5	−13.3	−12.2

DS...dual sourcing

By imposing an emission tax, which is in our case 15% of the product price per unit, the offshore order quantity and thereby also the carbon emissions from transport are reduced by 4.6%, 14.8% and 26.2% for σ_1, σ_2 and σ_3, respectively. But also the expected profit is reduced by 12.2% to 14.5%. The negative impact on the expected profit is higher for products with lower demand variability. This is intuitive as for products with low demand variability it makes sense to rely to a large extent on the offshore supplier; by being not allowed to order from the cost-efficient source the economic performance is more stongly harmed.

In order to show the impact of an increasing transport emission tax on the optimal decision the emission tax t is varied. The emission cost is varied in the range $0 \leq t < d$. Figures 4.4(a), 4.4(b) and 4.4(c) show the results including offshore order quantity, expected onshore order quantity and total

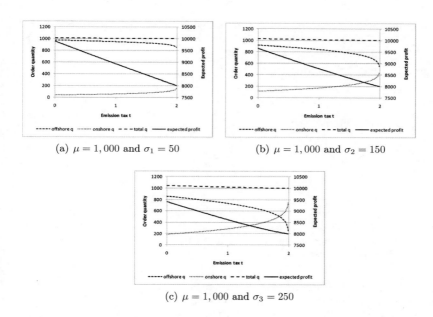

(a) $\mu = 1,000$ and $\sigma_1 = 50$

(b) $\mu = 1,000$ and $\sigma_2 = 150$

(c) $\mu = 1,000$ and $\sigma_3 = 250$

Figure 4.4: Offshore, onshore and total order quantity and expected profit depending on t

order quantity as well as expected profit depending on emission tax t for the three demand distributions. It is clearly shown that with increasing emission tax t the offshore order quantity decreases and the expected onshore order quantity increases. As a result, the total order quantity converges to the mean demand, see (4.12). First, the offshore order quantity decreases nearly linearly; as t is close to d it decreases more rapidly. For $t \geq d$, the offshore supplier is not used at all. The expected profit also decreases nearly linearly with increasing emission tax.

Figure 4.5 shows the percentage change of the transport carbon emissions and the expected profit depending on increasing emission tax t compared to the basic dual sourcing model. For products with low demand variability the relative reduction of transport carbon emissions is smaller than the relative decrease of expected profit. So, if policy-makers also pay attention to the economic impact of a policy instrument a transport carbon emission tax would not be a suitable option if it is applied to companies ordering products with a low demand variability from an offshore supplier. In contrast to this, for products with higher demand variability the relative reduction of transport carbon emissions always outweighs the reduction of expected profit. In this case, of course, the economic performance is also harmed by the introduction of an emission tax but the reduction of expected profit is accompanied by a high decrease of transport carbon emissions.

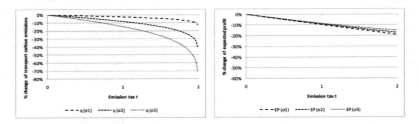

Figure 4.5: Dual sourcing with emission tax compared to basic dual sourcing: % change of transport carbon emissions (left) and expected profit (right) depending on t

The difference between the relative change of expected profit and the relative change of transport carbon emissions depending on t is graphically shown in Figure 4.6. If the difference is positive the relative reduction of transport carbon emissions outweighs the relative decrease of expected profit which can be considered as a good compromise for companies.

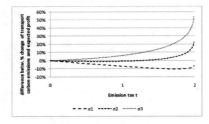

Figure 4.6: Dual sourcing with emission tax compared to basic dual sourcing: difference between % change of expected profit and % change of transport carbon emissions depending on t

In addition to comparing the dual sourcing model with and without emission tax it is of interest to compare the dual sourcing model with transport emission tax and the single offshore sourcing model. When assuming an emission tax $t = 1.5$ in the dual sourcing model the expected profit is even lower than in the case of single offshore sourcing. The results of these two models are shown in Table 4.9. The expected profit is reduced by 13.1%, 9.0% and 4.4%

for σ_1, σ_2 and σ_3, respectively. Even though the economic performance of the company is even reduced below the level of single offshoring it has to be pointed out that the impact on the environmental performance is extremely positive. The offshore order quantity and the related transport carbon emissions are reduced drastically, by 9.3%, 26.8% and 42.8% for σ_1, σ_2 and σ_3, respectively, when using dual sourcing with a linear emission tax instead of single offshore sourcing. It can be seen that the offshore order quantity and the transport carbon emissions decrease overproportionally for products with high demand variability.

Table 4.9: Comparison of single offshore sourcing and dual sourcing with emission tax $t = 1.5$

	σ_1	σ_2	σ_3
Offshore order q – single offshoring	1022	1065	1108
Offshore order q – DS with emission tax	927	780	634
Difference in %	−9.3	−26.8	−42.8
Expected profit – single offshoring	9727	9182	8637
Expected profit – DS with emission tax	8452	8357	8261
Difference in %	−13.1	−9.0	−4.4

DS... dual sourcing

For illustration purposes we calculate a "break-even" transport carbon emission tax which is the tax level with which the dual sourcing model yields the same or a higher expected profit than the single offshore sourcing model, i.e. $P_t(q^t) \geq P_{cl}(q_{cl}^*)$. This helps us to show which percentage of transport carbon emissions could be reduced without letting the economic performance fall below the values of the single offshoring sourcing. The results are shown in Table 4.10. For the given transport carbon emission tax, a reduction of 5.3% to 33.2% is possible depending on the demand distribution. For products with low demand variability only a very low emission tax level of $t = 0.1585$ could be implemented without decreasing the expected profit of dual sourcing below the expected profit of single offshore sourcing. For products with high demand variability the emission tax can be up to $t = 0.9573$.

Overall, it can be seen that the negative environmental impact of transport can be reduced with a dual sourcing strategy compared to a single offshore sourcing strategy. It becomes even more environmentally friendly if a transport emission tax is included into the decision as the offshore order quantity decreases with increasing emission tax t. But as a negative side-effect the expected profit of the company is also reduced.

Table 4.10: Comparison of single offshore sourcing and dual sourcing with "break-even" emission tax

	σ_1	σ_2	σ_3
"Break-even" emission tax	0.1585	0.5135	0.9573
Offshore order q – single offshoring	1022	1065	1108
Offshore order q – DS with emission tax	968	880	740
Difference in %	−5.3	−17.4	−33.2

DS...dual sourcing

4.5.4 Dual sourcing model with emission trading for transport

In the dual sourcing model including emission trading first the lower and upper control limits are computed with the emission buying price $b = 1.5$ and the emission selling price $s = 0.5$. The results are summarized in Table 4.11.

Table 4.11: Dual sourcing with emission trading: Lower and upper control limits

	σ_1	σ_2	σ_3
Lower control limit q^b	927	780	634
Upper control limit q^s	960	881	802

It has to be noted that that the control limits can be computed independently of the emission limit L. But the value of the emission limit L has a decisive impact on the optimal decision and the expected profit. Three different cases can be identified depending on the emission limit L. As long as $L < q^b \leq q^s$ the optimal order quantity equals to the lower control limit q^b. For $q^b \leq L \leq q^s$ the optimal order quantity equals to the emission limit L. As soon as $L > q^s \geq q^b$ the optimal order quantity is q^s. To illustrate this, we take three different emission limits (low, medium, high) for each of the three demand scenarios. The results of the calculations in comparison to the basic dual souring model are summarized in Table 4.12 showing the optimal offshore order quantity and the resulting expected profit for each case.

By comparing these results to the basic dual sourcing model without environmental regulations it can be seen that the offshore order quantity with emission trading is always lower than the offshore order quantity in the basic model. This is simply due to the fact that $q^L \leq q^*$ because additional cost parameters, i.e. the emission buying price b and the emission selling price s, are considered. The introduction of emission trading helps to limit the offshore order quantity to at least q^s, i.e. maximal offshore order quantity, irrespective of the emission limit L. This results in a reduction of transport carbon

Table 4.12: Optimal offshore order quantity and resulting expected profit for three values of emission limit L

(a) $\mu = 1000$ and $\sigma_1 = 50$

	Emission limit L	Offshore q (% change compared to basic DS model)	Expected profit (% change compared to basic DS model)
Low	$L = 800$	927 (-4.6)	9652 (-2.3)
Medium	$L = 950$	950 (-2.2)	9871 (-0.1)
High	$L = 1000$	960 (-1.2)	9898 ($+0.2$)

(b) $\mu = 1000$ and $\sigma_2 = 150$

	Emission limit L	Offshore q (% change compared to basic DS model)	Expected profit (% change compared to basic DS model)
Low	$L = 600$	780 (-14.8)	9257 (-4.0)
Medium	$L = 850$	850 (-7.1)	9613 (-0.3)
High	$L = 1000$	881 (-3.7)	9694 ($+0.5$)

(c) $\mu = 1000$ and $\sigma_3 = 250$

	Emission limit L	Offshore q (% change compared to basic DS model)	Expected profit (% change compared to basic DS model)
Low	$L = 400$	634 (-26.2)	8861 (-5.8)
Medium	$L = 750$	750 (-12.7)	9354 (-0.5)
High	$L = 1000$	802 (-6.6)	9490 ($+0.9$)

emissions of 1.2%, 3.7% or 6.6% for $s = 0.5$ and σ_1, σ_2 and σ_3, respectively. The maximal reduction of transport carbon emissions which can be achieved when q^b is ordered is between 4.6% and 26.2% for $b = 1.5$ depending on the demand scenario. For low emission limits, the expected profit is reduced by 2.3% to 5.8% while for high emission limits, even a slight increase of the expected profit by 0.2% to 0.9% can be achieved. Figures 4.7(a), 4.7(b) and 4.7(c) show how the profit curves develop depending on the offshore order quantity for a selected demand distribution ($\mu = 1000$ and $\sigma_2 = 150$) and the three cases of the emission limit L (low, medium, high).

The curve which shows the development of the expected profit $P_L(q)$ depending on the offshore order quantity is composed of the two curves $P_b(q)$ and $P_s(q)$ whereby depending on the emission limit different parts of the profit

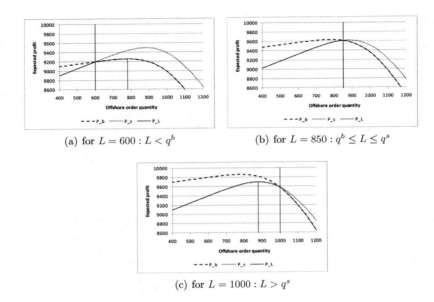

(a) for $L = 600 : L < q^b$

(b) for $L = 850 : q^b \leq L \leq q^s$

(c) for $L = 1000 : L > q^s$

Figure 4.7: Dual sourcing with emission trading: Expected profit depending on offshore order quantity for normally distributed demand with $\mu = 1000$ and $\sigma_2 = 150$

curves are realized, see also (4.18). For low emission limits, i.e. $L < q^b$, the expected profit $P_b(q)$ is generated while for high emission limits, i.e. $L > q^s$, the expected profit $P_s(q)$ is realized. For medium emission limits, an offshore order quantity equal to L is ordered and the expected profit $P(L) = P_b(L) = P_s(L)$ is generated, see also (4.21).

In Figures 4.8(a), 4.8(b) and 4.8(c) the off- and onshore order quantities depending on the emission limit L are presented.

Depending on the value of the emission limit L the impact can be positive or negative compared to the basic dual sourcing model. It is intuitive that a higher emission limit L leads to a higher expected profit because either less emission allowances have to be bought or more emission allowances can be sold. Figures 4.9(a), 4.9(b) and 4.9(c) demonstrate that the expected profit increases with the emission limit L. Furthermore, the expected profit of the basic dual sourcing model is included. For low and high emission limits the expected profit runs linearly whereby the slope directly depends on the value of b and s.

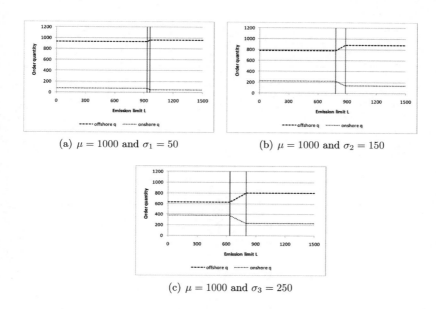

(a) $\mu = 1000$ and $\sigma_1 = 50$ (b) $\mu = 1000$ and $\sigma_2 = 150$

(c) $\mu = 1000$ and $\sigma_3 = 250$

Figure 4.8: Off- and onshore order quantity depending on L

Depending on the emission limit L the economic performance of the company can be better or worse than in the single offshore sourcing model and in the basic dual sourcing model without environmental regulations. For given values of s and b we can compute "break-even" emission limits under which the company yields the same or a higher expected profit than with single offshore sourcing or with basic dual sourcing, i.e. $P_L(q^L) \geq P_{cl}(q^*_{cl})$ or $P_L(q^L) \geq P(q^*)$, respectively. These "break-even" values indicate a pareto-optimal solution where the environmental performance is improved without sacrificing economic performance. We already calculated a "break-even" emission tax in the previous section but in that case only in comparison to single offshore sourcing because the introduction of an emission tax always leads to a reduction of expected profit compared to the basic dual sourcing model. The results for the "break-even" emission limits for the three demand scenarios are summarized in Table 4.13.

Compared to single offshore sourcing the "break-even" emission limit can be rather low. The same or a higher expected profit can be achieved in the dual sourcing model with emission trading even though emission allowances have to be bought in order to procure the optimal offshore order quantity q^L. The

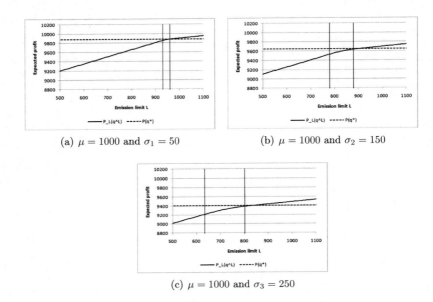

(a) $\mu = 1000$ and $\sigma_1 = 50$

(b) $\mu = 1000$ and $\sigma_2 = 150$

(c) $\mu = 1000$ and $\sigma_3 = 250$

Figure 4.9: Expected profit depending on L

transport carbon emissions can be reduced by 9.3% to 42.8%. In contrast to this, compared to the basic dual sourcing model, the same or a higher expected profit can only be achieved if the company is allowed to generate some revenue through the selling of emission allowances, which is the case when $L > q^s$. The transport carbon emissions can be slightly reduced by 1.2% to 6.7% while generating the same or a higher expected profit as in the basic dual sourcing model.

Varying the values of the prices for emission allowances, s and b, changes the upper and lower control limit whereby increasing values lead to decreasing limits. The difference between s and b determines the span between the lower and the upper control limit within which it is optimal for the company to order a quantity equal to L. But changing the emission prices has no direct impact on the optimal decision because the optimal offshore order quantity can only be determined together with a respective emission limit L.

For policy-making it is of interest that from the company's perspective there is a minimal offshore order quantity, i.e. q^b. Under emission trading the company never orders less than q^b from the offshore supplier even when emission allowances have to be bought for that. Therefore, for policy-making it does

Table 4.13: Dual sourcing with emission trading with "break-even" emission limit

(a) Compared to single offshore sourcing

	σ_1	σ_2	σ_3
"Break-even" emission limit	851	551	251
Offshore order q – single offshoring	1022	1065	1108
Offshore order q – DS with emission limit	927	780	634
Difference in %	−9.3	−26.8	−42.8

(b) Compared to basic dual sourcing

	σ_1	σ_2	σ_3
"Break-even" emission limit	967	899	832
Offshore order q – basic dual sourcing	972	915	859
Offshore order q – DS with emission limit	960	881	802
Difference in %	−1.2	−3.7	−6.7

DS... dual sourcing

not seem to be reasonable to set the emission limit L below q^b. An emission limit $L < q^b$ would not help to reduce transport carbon emissions but would only hurt the economic performance and competitiveness of the company.

Table 4.14: Dual sourcing with emission trading $L = q^b$: Optimal offshore order quantity and expected profit

	σ_1	σ_2	σ_3
Optimal offshore order quantity $L = q^b$	927	780	634
Difference to basic dual sourcing in %	−4.6	−14.8	−26.2
Difference to dual sourcing with $t = 1.5$ in %	0	0	0
Expected profit with $L = q^b$	9840	9527	9206
Difference to basic dual sourcing in %	−0.4	−1.2	−2.1
Difference to dual sourcing with $t = 1.5$ in %	+16.4	+14.0	+11.4

The results for the dual sourcing model with an emission limit $L = q^b$ are summarized in Table 4.14. The results are compared to the basic dual sourcing model and to the dual sourcing model with an emission tax. From the perspective of policy-making, by setting $L = q^b$ the maximal reduction of transport carbon emissions which is possible under an emission trading scheme is reached. Compared to the basic dual sourcing model the transport carbon emissions are reduced by 4.6% to 26.2%. Compared to basic dual sourcing, it seems that an emission limit $L = q^b$ is also compatible from the company's perspective as it does not significantly harm the economic performance; the expected profit is only reduced by 0.4%, 1.2% and 2.1% for σ_1, σ_2 and σ_3, respectively. Furthermore, if the company had to choose between a transport emission tax and emission trading the company would be much better off with an emission trading scheme for transport. Assuming an emission tax equal to the emission buying price, i.e. $b = t = 1.5$, the expected profit can be improved by 16.4%, 14.0% and 11.4% for σ_1, σ_2 and σ_3, respectively.

For the further sensitivity analyses with the dual sourcing model with emission trading we set the emission selling price $s = 0$ and the emission limit to $L = q^b$ which can be considered as a reasonable emission limit from the perspective of policy and management. The emission buying price b is varied in the range $0 \leq b < d$. The development of the optimal offshore order quantity and the expected profit for the demand scenarios is depicted in Figure 4.10.

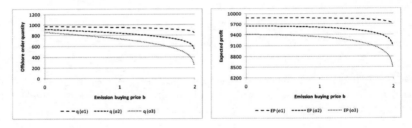

Figure 4.10: Dual sourcing with emission trading $L = q^b$: Optimal offshore order quantity (left) and expected profit (right) depending on b

The optimal offshore order quantity decreases with increasing b. A similar development of the offshore order quantity has already been shown for the dual sourcing model with an emission tax (see Figure 4.4). But in contrast to the dual sourcing model with an emission tax where the expected profit decreases rapidly and nearly linearly with increasing emission tax t the expected profit in the dual sourcing model with emission trading is less sensitive to increasing values of the emission buying price b. This indicates that under emission trading the economic performance is less strongly harmed by an increasing emission buying price b.

Figure 4.11 shows the relative difference of transport carbon emissions and the expected profit of the dual sourcing model with emission trading compared to the basic dual sourcing model. It is straightforward that the expected profit is lower in the dual sourcing model with emission trading than in the basic dual sourcing model without environmental regulations. This is simply because additional costs are introduced and the company has to deviate from the optimal decision q^* which does not consider the environmental dimension. However, it has to be noted that the relative reduction of transport carbon emissions outweighs the relative decrease of the expected profit for $L = q^b$. In other words, the environmental improvement is greater than the degradation with respect to economic performance. The transport carbon emissions can be reduced by up to 12.4%, 39.6% and 70.4% for σ_1, σ_2 and σ_3, respectively. In contrast to this, the company only has to accept a decrease of expected profit of up to 1.8%, 5.6% and 9.5% for σ_1, σ_2 and σ_3, respectively. This is a significant difference to the dual sourcing model with an emission tax.

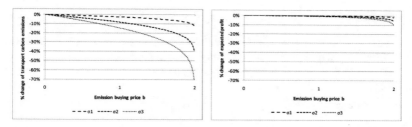

Figure 4.11: Dual sourcing with emission trading $L = q^b$ compared to basic dual sourcing: % change of transport carbon emissions (left) and expected profit (right) depending on b

With an emission tax, the relative improvement with respect to transport carbon emissions only outweighs the relative decrease of expected profit for products with high demand variability. Companies ordering products with low demand variability for which the cheap, offshore supplier is more important suffer more strongly by an introduction of an emission tax (see Figure 4.6). This fact indicates that different companies are treated rather equally by emission trading in contrast to an emission tax.

In order to compare the dual sourcing model with emission trading and the dual sourcing model with an emission tax we assume that the emission buying price and the emission tax are the same, i.e. $b = t$. The emission buying price b is varied in the range $0 \leq b < d$. Due to $b = t$, under both regulations the same quantity $q^b = q^t$ is ordered. So the two models have the same performance with respect to transport carbon emissions. But there is a significant difference with respect to economic performance. The dual sourcing model with emission trading always outperforms the dual sourcing model with an emission tax with respect to expected profit. The relative difference between the expected profit of the dual sourcing model with emission trading and the basic model is shown in Figure 4.12.

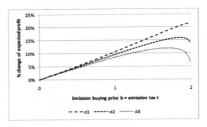

Figure 4.12: Dual sourcing with emission trading $L = q^b$ compared to dual sourcing with emission tax $t = b$: % change of expected profit depending on b

Overall, it can be seen that emission trading can help to improve the environmental performance of the company compared to single offshore sourcing and the basic dual sourcing model. When the emission limit is reasonably set the company can nearly keep its economic performance and competitiveness while strongly reducing the negative environmental impact from transport.

4.6 Comparison of the models and implications for management and policy-making

The summary of the numerical analyses of the basic models and its extensions is presented in Tables 4.15(a), 4.15(b) and 4.15(c). For each model the optimal offshore order quantity and the expected profit are given. We compare the results for the single offshore sourcing model, the basic dual sourcing model, the dual sourcing model with an emission tax and the dual sourcing model with emission trading for the three demand scenarios. For the dual sourcing model with emission trading different values of the emission limit L are assumed, namely low, medium and high and $L = q^b$. The basic dual sourcing model without environmental regulations is taken as point of reference for all the other models.

By comparing single offshore sourcing and basic dual sourcing (see columns 2 and 3 in Table 4.15) it can be seen that simply by using a dual sourcing strategy the negative environmental impact from transport can be reduced while simultaneously economic performance can be improved. The offshore order quantity is reduced when dual sourcing is used instead of single offshore sourcing. Thereby, the transport carbon emissions can be lowered as well.

The improvement potential with respect to economic and environmental performance is larger for products with higher demand variability. This is due

Table 4.15: Summary of results of the different models

(a) $\mu = 1000$ and $\sigma_1 = 50$

	Single Offshore	Basic DS model	DS with $t = 1.5$	DS with $L = 800$ $b = 1.5$ $s = 0.5$	DS with $L = 950$ $b = 1.5$ $s = 0.5$	DS with $L = 1000$ $b = 1.5$ $s = 0.5$	DS with $L = q^b$ $b = 1.5$ $s = 0.5$
Offshore order q	1022	972	927	927	950	960	927
Difference in %	+5.1	0.0	−4.6	−4.6	−2.3	−1.2	−4.6
Expected profit	9727	9881	8452	9652	9871	9898	9842
Difference in %	−1.6	0.0	−14.5	−2.3	−0.1	+0.1	−0.4

(b) $\mu = 1000$ and $\sigma_2 = 150$

	Single Offshore	Basic DS model	DS with $t = 1.5$	DS with $L = 600$ $b = 1.5$ $s = 0.5$	DS with $L = 850$ $b = 1.5$ $s = 0.5$	DS with $L = 1000$ $b = 1.5$ $s = 0.5$	DS with $L = q^b$ $b = 1.5$ $s = 0.5$
Offshore order q	1065	915	780	780	850	881	780
Difference in %	+16.4	0.0	−14.8	−14.8	−7.1	−3.7	−14.8
Expected profit	9182	9643	8357	9257	9613	9694	9527
Difference in %	−4.8	0.0	−13.3	−4.0	−0.3	+0.5	−1.2

(c) $\mu = 1000$ and $\sigma_3 = 250$

	Single Offshore	Basic DS model	DS with $t = 1.5$	DS with $L = 400$ $b = 1.5$ $s = 0.5$	DS with $L = 750$ $b = 1.5$ $s = 0.5$	DS with $L = 1000$ $b = 1.5$ $s = 0.5$	DS with $L = q^b$ $b = 1.5$ $s = 0.5$
Offshore order q	1108	859	634	634	750	802	634
Difference in %	+29.0	0.0	−26.2	−26.2	−12.7	−6.6	−26.2
Expected profit	8637	9405	8261	8861	9354	9490	9212
Difference in %	−8.2	0.0	−12.2	−5.8	−0.5	+0.90	−2.1

DS...dual sourcing
q...quantity

to the fact the for these products the switch from a single, slow and inflexible supplier to two suppliers of which one is fast and flexible provides more value. This means that the company is more willing to use the onshore supplier and the expected profit can be improved more strongly than for products with low demand variability. Dual sourcing becomes even more environmentally friendly if regulations for transport carbon emissions are included. The considered environmental regulations help to control the company's decision to some extent and the transport carbon emissions can be further reduced. However, the impact on the expected profit can be positive or negative depending on the regulatory measure and the policy parameters.

The introduction of an emission tax for the transport from the offshore supplier narrows the cost advantage of the offshore supplier and therefore induces the company to reduce its offshore order quantity compared to the basic dual sourcing model. Thereby, the transport carbon emissions can be further lowered which improves the environmental performance of the company. But at the same time the economic performance of the company is severely harmed and the expected profit falls below the value of the basic dual sourcing model. The expected profit in the dual sourcing model with emission tax is also lower than in the single offshore sourcing model for an emission tax $t = 1.5$ (see column 4 in Table 4.15). Lower values of the emission tax, of course, have less impact on the expected profit; up to a certain value of the emission tax t dual sourcing with an emission tax can outperform the single offshore sourcing model with respect to expected profit. The "break-even" emission tax under which dual sourcing with emission tax and single offshore sourcing yield the same expected profit can take a higher value for products with higher demand variability (see Table 4.10). This is due to the fact that companies procuring products with low demand variability from a cheap offshore supplier are more sensitive to the introduction of an emission tax for the transport from this source. If an emission trading system for transport is introduced, the ordering decision of the company is affected as well. When considering a buying and a selling price for emission allowances and $b \geq s$ the optimal decision is given by a two-sided control limit policy. The results for three different emission limits (low, medium, high) are shown in columns 5, 6 and 7 in Table 4.15. Irrespective of the emission limit L, a reduction of the offshore order quantity and the related transport carbon emissions can always be achieved with the introduction of emission trading for transport compared to single offshore sourcing and the basic dual sourcing model because $q^L \leq q^* \leq q_{cl}^*$.

Low emission limits lead to a reduction of the expected profit compared to the basic dual sourcing model. However, the relative reduction of the offshore order quantity and the related transport emissions is always larger than the relative reduction of the expected profit. For medium to high emission limits, only a slight decrease of the expected profit has to be accepted compared to the basic dual sourcing model. Even an increase of the profit can be achieved when enough emission allowances can be sold due to a high emission limit. But the influence of emission trading on the ordering decision and thereby on the environmental improvement is limited. As the company never orders less than q^b an emission limit below that value does not improve the environmental performance of the company. Setting the emission limit to $L = q^b$ (see column 8 of Table 4.15) seems to be compatible for the company with respect to economic and environmental performance; compared to the basic dual sourcing model the expected profit is almost the same but transport emissions can be reduced considerably. In Table 4.14 (column 8) a reduction between approx. 4.6% and 26.2% is shown. With an emission tax of $t = b = 1.5$ the same reduction of transport carbon emissions could be achieved. However, it has to be noted that the expected profit in the dual sourcing with emission trading is considerably higher. Compared to dual sourcing with an emission tax, the expected profit in the dual sourcing model with emission trading can be increased by approx. 11.4% to 16.4% (see Table 4.14). This result indicates that emission trading is preferred to an emission tax from the company perspective.

Also from the perspective of policy-making, it can be concluded that the emission limit should be set to q^b. Thereby the negative environmental impact of transport can be reduced and the company can still achieve a considerably high profit. Policy-makers have to be aware of the fact that the minimal offshore order quantity q^b strongly depends on the demand distribution F and on the emission buying price b, see (4.19). Setting $L = q^b$ and using (4.19) results in the following relation between the emission limit L and the emission buying price b:

$$b = d \cdot (1 - F(L)) - (c - z)F(L) \qquad (4.23)$$

This shows the basic relation between the parameters: b decreases as L increases. Also, Hua et al. (2011) point out that emission price could be modeled as a decreasing function of the emission cap, i.e. emission limit. For the offshore order quantity equal to L (4.23) describes the difference between the expected onshore ordering costs per unit $d \cdot (1 - F(L))$ and the expected offshore ordering costs $(c - z)F(L)$. In newsvendor terminology it is the difference of the expected cost of understocking and the expected cost of overstocking for the basic dual sourcing model. Thus, the emission buying price b and the emission limit L should be fixed by considering the economic situation of the industry which is expressed by the offshore product cost, the onshore product cost and the market demand of the product reflected by the demand distribution F. If the policy parameters are fixed in the described manner, the economic and the environmental performance of the company can be balanced by achieving a high reduction of transport carbon emissions while generating a satisfying expected profit.

Chapter 5

Conclusions, limitations and further research opportunities

Our work aims to contribute to an emerging field of research which deals with the trade-off between economic and environmental performance of supply chains. Supply chains consist of all processes, such as sourcing, production, transport and warehousing, which are necessary to deliver products to the final customer. The main goal of traditional supply chain management is to design the supply chain processes so that the customer requests are fulfilled at low costs. In general, there is a trade-off between efficiency and responsiveness. For instance, it is not possible to minimize inventory costs while simultaneously maximizing product availability. Several drivers influence the efficiency and responsiveness of supply chains and these drivers have to be designed to align the supply chain strategy with the competitive strategy.

In recent years, in addition to traditional economic performance measures, such as cost or profit and customer service, other criteria have become important as well which leads to reconsidering existing supply chain strategies. Especially the impact of supply chains on sustainability is a highly discussed topic at the moment. Sustainability includes the three dimensions, economic, environmental and social sustainability. In particular, the environment has received increasing attention from society, customers and authorities due to global problems, such as the depletion of natural resources, acidification or climate change. Carbon emissions which are produced through the burning of fossil fuels are assumed to be one of the main contributors to climate change. Therefore, international agreements, such as the Kyoto protocol, aim at the reduction of carbon emissions and other greenhouse gases in order to stop global warming. Based on that, environmental regulations have already been and will be implemented which limit the output of carbon emissions. These regulations also have an impact on supply chains and, in particular, their production, sourcing and transportation decisions. In Europe, for heavy, energy-intensive industries the EU emission trading scheme was introduced in 2005 with the aim of limiting and reducing the carbon emissions of certain sectors. Behind energy-intensive industries, transport is the second largest "polluter" in the EU. It is likely that also the transport sector might be confronted with new regulations, such as carbon emission limits, carbon emission taxes or emission trading for transport, on a European or even global scale.

Due to that, in the future, companies have to consider the environment and related regulations in decision-making. Research is needed in order to evaluate the impact of supply chains on the environment and to investigate the impact of regulations on the performance of supply chains. To contribute to this field of research, Chapter 2 deals with the basics of supply chain management and the relations between supply chains and the environment. Then an overview of models which integrate the environmental dimension in decision-making is provided in Chapter 3. It turns out that the environmental dimension can be integrated into decision-making by including environmental costs in the objective function, by (a) adding constraint(s) which reflect the environmental concerns or by relying on multi-objective programming approaches to balance economic and environmental goals.

We want to contribute to this field of research by analysing the economic and environmental sustainability of dual sourcing in contrast to single (offshore) sourcing. We build on the single-period dual sourcing model with an offshore and an onshore source based on the newsvendor framework. With single offshore sourcing the company can order only once before the selling season. In contrast to this, dual sourcing allows the company to order from a cheap, offshore supplier before the selling season and in addition to that from an expensive, onshore supplier which serves as a backup during the season. The economic performance is evaluated with the expected profit and the customer service whereby it is shown that dual sourcing with an offshore and an onshore supplier helps to increase both performance measures. In addition to that, we consider the transport carbon emissions which are produced when ordering from the offshore supplier as environmental criterion. The transport carbon emissions are directly related to the offshore order quantity which means that a lower offshore order quantity automatically leads to lower transport carbon emissions and improved environmental performance. It turns out that simply by switching from a single offshore sourcing strategy to dual sourcing the economic and the environmental performance can be simultaneously improved.

In addition to that we model different environmental regulations which could be valid for the transport sector in the future and analyse their impact on the company's decision and its economic and environmental performance. In order to be able to model the different regulations, of course, we have to abstract from reality and we relate the environmental regulations to one product unit. So, the reader has to be aware that our results only give indications about how companies might react to the introduction of different regulations concerning transport carbon emissions and are not directly transferable to a real-world setting.

Firstly, we assume that a strict emission limit in the form of emission allowances per product unit is imposed. This restricts the offshore order quantity and the related transport carbon emissions. Of course, a strict emission limit has a negative impact on the company's economic performance when it restrains the company from ordering the profit-maximizing offshore order quantity. But at the same time the transport carbon emissions can be reduced. Depending on the value of the limit, the cost and price parameters and the demand distribution, the relative improvement on the environmental dimension can outweigh the relative degradation of the economic performance.

Secondly, we assume that a linear emission tax is imposed on transport from the offshore source. The transport emission tax reduces the cost advantage of the offshore supplier and therefore induces the company to order less from the offshore supplier. So, an emission tax also helps to reduce the transport carbon emissions but at the same time severely harms the economic performance of the company; the negative impact is particularly large for companies ordering products with low demand variability.

Thirdly, we assume that an emission trading scheme for transport is implemented. This means that the company receives a certain amount of emission allowances, i.e. emission limit, free of charge which are then used to cover the carbon emissions related to the transport activity from the offshore supplier. Additional emission allowances have to be bought if the transport activity is too high or can be sold if not all emission allowances have been used. We show that with emission trading the offshore order quantity and the related transport emissions can be reduced and at the same time the economic performance measures are nearly not harmed. So, emission trading seems to be compatible from policy and company perspective as it helps to reduce the negative environmental impact of company's decision while not significantly harming the company's economic performance.

Our work helps to gain insights into new trade-offs which arise if in addition to economic criteria also environmental ones are considered. It can provide decision support for individual companies on how much to order from a certain supply source. Furthermore, we model different regulation schemes and therefore, our model can also be used to derive implications for policy-making with respect of the design of environmental regulations. But, it has to be noted that our work is only one of the first steps in a new and emerging field of research. Our work also provides a starting point for further research opportunities. It has been shown that the parameters of the regulations, i.e. the emission tax, the emission limit and the prices of the emission allowances, are critical values. So further research is needed into how these parameters can be reasonably set and how they influence each other. For instance, the prices for emission allowances are not set by policy but determined by the market as a function of the emission limit. So the emission prices could be modelled as a decreasing function of the emission limit or with the help of a probability distribution reflecting the stochasticity of these prices. Furthermore, new developments of emission trading, such as the auctioning of emission allowances, could be considered in further research.

Bibliography

Abdallah, T., Diabat, A., Simchi-Levi, D., 2010. A carbon sensitive supply chain network problem with green procurement. In: Proceedings of the 40th International Conference on Computers and Industrial Engineering. pp. 1–6.

Allon, G., van Mieghem, J. A., 2010. Global dual sourcing: Tailored base-surge allocation to near- and offshore production. Management Science 56 (1), 110–124.

Anciaux, D., Yuan, K., 2007. Green supply chain: Intermodal transportation modeling with environmental impacts. In: Proceedings of the European Transport Conference 2007.

Angell, L. C., Klassen, R. D., 1999. Integrating environmental issues into the mainstream: An agenda for research in operations management. Journal of Operations Management 17 (5), 575–598.

Antes, R., Hansjürgens, B., Letmathe, P. (Eds.), 2008. Emission Trading: Institutional Design, Decision Making and Corporate Strategies. Springer.

Anthony, R., 1965. Planning and control systems. Harvard University.

Anupindi, R., Chopra, S., Deshmukh, S., van Mieghem, J., Zemel, E., 2006. Managing Business Process Flows – Principles of Operations Management. Pearson Prentice Hall.

Anvari, M., 1987. Optimality criteria and risk in inventory models: The case of the newsboy problem. The Journal of the Operational Research Society 38 (7), 625–632.

Barankin, E., 1961. A delivery-lag inventory model with an emergency provision (the single-period case). Naval Research Logistics Quarterly 8 (3), 285–311.

Benjaafar, S., Li, Y., Daskin, M., 2010. Carbon footprints and the management of supply chains: Insights from simple models. Working Paper, University of Minnesota.

Berger, P. D., Gerstenfeld, A., Zeng, A. Z., 2004. How many suppliers are best? A decision-analysis approach. Omega 32 (1), 9–15.

Berger, P. D., Zeng, A.-Z., 2006. Single versus multiple sourcing in the presence of risks. Journal of the Operational Research Society 57 (3), 250–261.

Bloemhof-Ruwaard, J., van Nunen, J. A. E. E., 2005. Integration of environmental management and SCM. Online.
URL http://papers.ssrn.com/sol3/papers.cfm?abstract_id=902503

Bloemhof-Ruwaard, J. M., van Beek, P., Hordijk, L., van Wassenhove, L. N., 1995. Interactions between operational research and environmental management. European Journal of Operational Research 85 (2), 229–243.

Bloemhof-Ruwaard, J. M., van Wassenhove, L. N., Gabel, H. L., Weaver, P., 1996. An environmental life cycle optimization model for the European pulp and paper industry. Omega 24 (6), 615–629.

Bojarski, A. D., Laínez, J. M., Espuña, A., Puigjaner, L., 2009. Incorporating environmental impacts and regulations in a holistic supply chains modeling: An LCA approach. Computers & Chemical Engineering 33 (10), 1747–1759.

Bonney, M., 2009. Inventory planning to help the environment. In: Jaber, M. Y. (Ed.), Inventory Management: Non-Classical Views. Taylor & Francis Ltd., pp. 43–74.

Bonney, M., Jaber, M. Y., 2010. Environmentally responsible inventory models: Non-classical models for a non-classical era. International Journal of Production Economics (In Press, Corrected Proof), –.

BSI Group, 2010. PAS 2050. Online.
URL http://www.bsigroup.com/Standards-and-Publications/How-we-can-help-you/Professional-Standards-Service/PAS-2050

Burke, G. J., Carrillo, J. E., Vakharia, A. J., 2007. Single versus multiple supplier sourcing strategies. European Journal of Operational Research 182 (1), 95–112.

Burke Jr., G. J., 2005. Sourcing strategies in a supply chain. Ph.D. thesis, Unversity of Florida.

Cachon, G., Terwiesch, C., 2009. Matching Supply with Demand – An Introduction to Operations Management. McGraw-Hill.

Cadarso, M.-A., López, L.-A., Gómez, N., Tobarra, M.-A., 2010. CO2 emissions of international freight transport and offshoring: Measurement and allocation. Ecological Economics 69 (8), 1682–1694.

Carter, C. R., Rogers, D. S., 2008. A framework of sustainable supply chain management: Moving toward new theory. International Journal of Physical Distribution & Logistics Management 38 (5), 360–387.

Chen, C., Monahan, G. E., 2010. Environmental safety stock: The impacts of regulatory and voluntary control policies on production planning, inventory control, and environmental performance. European Journal of Operational Research 207 (3), 1280–1292.

Chen, X., Sim, M., Simchi-Levi, D., Sun, P., 2007. Risk aversion in inventory management. Operations Research 55 (5), 828–842.

Choi, T.-M., Chow, P.-S., 2008. Mean-variance analysis of quick response program. International Journal of Production Economics 114 (2), 456–475.

Cholette, S., Venkat, K., 2009. The energy and carbon intensity of wine distribution: A study of logistical options for delivering wine to consumers. Journal of Cleaner Production 17 (16), 1401–1413.

Chopra, S., Meindl, P., 2010. Supply Chain Management – Strategy, Planning & Operations. Pearson.

Chung, C.-S., Flynn, J., Kirca, Ö., 2008. A multi-item newsvendor problem with preseason production and capacitated reactive production. European Journal of Operational Research 188 (3), 775–792.

Chung, K. H., 1990. Risk in inventory models: The case of the newsboy problem – optimality conditions. The Journal of the Operational Research Society 41 (2), 173–176.

Coase, R. H., 1960. The problem of social cost. Journal of Law and Economics 3 (October), 1–44.

Convery, F., 2009. Origins and Development of the EU ETS. Environmental and Resource Economics 43 (3), 391–412.

Corbett, C. J., Klassen, R. D., 2006. Extending the horizons: Environmental excellence as key to improving operations. Manufacturing & Service Operations Management 8 (1), 5–22.

Craig, A., Blanco, E., Sheffi, Y., 2009. Measuring supply chain carbon efficiency. In: Proceedings of POMS 20th Annual Meeting.

Crocker, T. D., 1966. The structuring of atmospheric pollution control systems. In: Wolozin, H. (Ed.), The Economics of Air Pollution. W. W. Norton & Co, pp. 61–86.

Cruz, J. M., 2008. Dynamics of supply chain networks with corporate social responsibility through integrated environmental decision-making. European Journal of Operational Research 184 (3), 1005–1031.

Cruz, J. M., Matsypura, D., 2009. Supply chain networks with corporate social responsibility through integrated environmental decision-making. International Journal of Production Research 47 (3), 621–648.

Cruz, J. M., Wakolbinger, T., 2008. Multiperiod effects of corporate social
responsibility on supply chain networks, transaction costs, emissions, and
risk. International Journal of Production Economics 116 (1), 61–74.

Dada, M., Petruzzi, N. C., Schwarz, L. B., 2007. A newsvendor's procurement
problem when suppliers are unreliable. Manufacturing & Service Operations
Management 9 (1), 9–32.

Dales, J. H., 1968. Pollution, property & prices: An essay in policy-making
and economics. University of Toronto Press.

Daniel, S., D.C., D., Pappis, C., 1997. Operations research and environmental
planning. European Journal of Operational Research 102 (2), 248–263.

Diabat, A., Simchi-Levi, D., 2009. A carbon-capped supply chain network
problem. In: Proceedings of the 2009 IEEE IEEM. pp. 523–527.

Dobos, I., 1998. Production-inventory control under environmental constraints.
International Journal of Production Economics 56-57 (1), 123–131.

Domschke, W., Scholl, A., 2005. Grundlagen der Betriebswirtschaftslehre –
Eine Einführung aus entscheidungsorientierter Sicht. Springer.

Dyckhoff, H., Lackes, R., Reese, J., 2004. Supply chain management and reverse logistics. Springer.

Ecoinvent, 2011. Ecoinvent database. Online.
    URL http://www.ecoinvent.ch/

EcoTransIT, 2010. EcoTransIT – Make your own calculation. Online.
    URL http://www.ecotransit.org/ecotransit.en.phtml

EEA, 2008. Greenhouse gas emission trends and projections in Europe 2008.
European Environment Agency.

EEA, 2009. Greenhouse gas emission trends and projections in Europe 2009.
European Environment Agency.

Eeckhoudt, L., Gollier, C., Schlesinger, H., 1995. The risk-averse (and prudent)
newsboy. Management Science 41 (5), 786–794.

Egenhofer, C., 2007. The making of the EU Emissions Trading Scheme: Status, prospects and implications for business. European Management Journal 25 (6), 453–463.

Ehrenfeld, J. R., 2005. The roots of sustainability. MIT Sloan Management Review 46 (2), 22–25.

Eisenkopf, A., 2008. Logistik und Umwelt. In: Arnold, D., Kuhn, A., Furmans, K., Isermann, H., Tempelmeier, H. (Eds.), Handbuch Logistik. Springer, pp. 1017–1050.

Elkington, J., 2004. Enter the triple bottom line. In: Henriques, A., Richardson, J. (Eds.), The Triple Bottom Line: Does It All Add Up? Earthscan, pp. 1–16.

European Commission, 2006. Building a global carbon market – Report pursuant to Article 30 of Directive 2003/87/EC.

European Commission, 2010a. Emissions trading: Questions and answers on the EU ETS auctioning regulation. Online.
URL http://europa.eu/rapid/pressReleasesAction.do?reference=MEMO/10/338&type=HTML

European Commission, 2010b. ILCD Handbook: General guide for life cycle assessment – provisions and action steps. Online.
URL http://lct.jrc.ec.europa.eu/pdf-directory/ILCD-Handbook-General-guide-for-LCA-DETAIL-online-12March2010.pdf

European Community, 2003a. Directive 2002/96/EC of the European Parliament and of the Council of 27 January 2003 on waste electrical and electronic equipment (WEEE). Online.
URL http://eur-lex.europa.eu/LexUriServ/LexUriServ.do?uri=CONSLEG:2002L0096:20080321:EN:PDF

European Community, 2003b. Directive 2008/87/EC of the European Parliament and the Council of 13 October 2003 establishing a scheme for greenhouse gas emissions trading within the Community and amending Council Directive 96/61/EC. Online.
URL http://eur-lex.europa.eu/LexUriServ/LexUriServ.do?uri=OJ:L:2003:275:0032:0046:EN:PDF

European Community, 2005. Questions and answers on emissions trading and national allocation plans. Online.
URL http://europa.eu/rapid/pressReleasesAction.do?reference=MEMO/05/84&format

European Community, 2008. Directive 2008/101/EC of the European Parliament and of the Council of 19 November 2008 amending Directive 2003/87/EC so as to include aviation activities in the scheme for greenhouse gas emission allowance trading within the Community. Online.
URL http://eur-lex.europa.eu/LexUriServ/LexUriServ.do?uri=OJ:L:2009:008:0003:0021:EN:PDF

Eurostat, 2009. Panorama of Transport. Online.
URL http://epp.eurostat.ec.europa.eu/cache/ITY_OFFPUB/KS-DA-09-001/EN/KS-DA-09-001-EN.PDF

Ferreira, J., Prokopets, L., 2009. Does offshoring still make sense? Supply Chain Management Review 13 (1), 20–27.

Fichtinger, J., 2010. The single-period inventory model with spectral risk measures. Ph.D. thesis, WU Vienna.

Fisher, M., Raman, A., 1996. Reducing the cost of demand uncertainty through accurate response to early sales. Operations Research 44 (1), 87–99.

Fisher, M. L., 1997. What is the right supply chain for your product? Harvard Business Review 75 (2), 105–116.

Flapper, S. D. P., van Nunen, J. A., Van Wassenhove, L. N. (Eds.), 2005. Managing Closed-Loop Supply Chains. Springer.

Fleischmann, B., Meyr, H., Wagner, M., 2008. Advanced planning. In: Stadtler, H., Kilger, C. (Eds.), Supply Chain Management and Advanced Planning. Springer, pp. 81–106.

Fleischmann, M., Bloemhof-Ruwaard, J. M., Dekker, R., van der Laan, E., van Nunen, J. A. E. E., van Wassenhove, L. N., 1997. Quantitative models for reverse logistics: A review. European Journal of Operational Research 103 (1), 1–17.

Gallego, G., Moon, I., 1993. The distribution free newsboy problem: Review and extensions. The Journal of the Operational Research Society 44 (8), 825–834.

Goedkoop, M., Spriensma, R., 2001. The Eco-indicator 99: A damage oriented method for Life Cycle Impact Assessment – Methodology Report. PRé Consultants B.V.

Golany, B., Yang, J., Yu, G., 2001. Economic lot-sizing with remanufacturing options. IIE Transactions 33 (11), 995–1003.

Goulder, L. H., Parry, I. W. H., Williams III, R. C., Burtraw, D., 1999. The cost-effectiveness of alternative instruments for environmental protection in a second-best setting. Journal of Public Economics 72 (3), 329–360.

Guide, V. Daniel R., J., Jayaraman, V., Srivastava, R., Benton, W. C., 2000. Supply-chain management for recoverable manufacturing systems. Interfaces 30 (3), 125–142.

Hagelaar, G. J. L. F., van der Vorst, J. G. A. J., 2002. Environmental supply chain management: Using life cycle assessment to structure supply chains. The International Food and Agribusiness Management Review 4 (4), 399–412.

Halldorsson, A., Kotzab, H., Skjott-Larsen, T., 2009. Supply chain management on the crossroad to sustainability: A blessing or a curse? Logistics Research 1 (2), 83–94.

Hillier, F. S., Lieberman, G. J., 2010. Introduction to operations research. McGraw-Hill.

Hoel, M., 1998. Emission taxes versus other environmental policies. The Scandinavian Journal of Economics 100 (1), 79–104.

Hoen, K., Tan, T., Fransoo, J., van Houtum, G., 2010. Effect of carbon emission regulations on transport mode selection in supply chains. Working Paper, Eindhoven University of Technology.

Holt, C. C., Modigliani, F., Muth, J. F., Simon, H. A., 1960. Planning Production, Inventory and Work Force. Prentice Hall.

Hou, J., Zeng, A. Z., Zhao, L., 2010. Coordination with a backup supplier through buy-back contract under supply disruption. Transportation Research Part E 46 (6), 881–895.

Hua, G., Cheng, T., Wang, S., 2011. Managing carbon footprints in inventory control. International Journal of Production Economics (In Press, Accepted Manuscript), –.

Huebler, M., 2009. Can carbon based import tariffs effectively reduce carbon emissions? Working Paper, Kiel Institute for the World Economy.

Hugo, A., Pistikopoulos, E., 2005. Environmentally conscious long-range planning and design of supply chain networks. Journal of Cleaner Production 13 (15), 1471–1491.

Huppes, G., Ishikawa, M., 2005. A framework for quantified eco-efficiency analysis. Journal of Industrial Ecology 9 (4), 25–41.

Huppes, G., Ishikawa, M., 2007. An introduction to quantified eco-efficiency analysis. In: Huppes, G., Ishikawa, M. (Eds.), Quantified Eco-Efficiency: An Introduction with Applications. Springer, pp. 1–38.

IEA, 2009. How the energy sector can deliver on a climate agreement in Copenhagen. International Energy Agency.

Inman, A. R., 1999. Environmental management: New challenges for production and inventory managers. Production and Inventory Managament Journal 40 (3), 46–49.

IPCC, 2007. IPCC Fourth Assessment Report. Online.
URL http://www.ipcc.ch/publications_and_data/publications_ipcc_fou rth_assessment_report_synthesis_report.htm

ISO, 2010. ISO 14 000. International Organization for Standardization.

Iyer, A. V., Bergen, M. E., 1997. Quick response in manufacturer-retailer channels. Management Science 43 (4), 559–570.

Jammernegg, W., Kischka, P., 2007. Risk-averse and risk-taking newsvendors: a conditional expected value approach. Review of Managerial Science 1 (1), 93–110.

Jammernegg, W., Kischka, P., 2009. Risk preferences and robust inventory decisions. International Journal of Production Economics 118 (1), 269–274.

Jolliet, O., Margni, M., Charles, R., Humbert, S., Payet, J., Rebitzer, G., Rosenbaum, R., 2003. Impact 2002+: A new life cycle impact assessment methodology. The International Journal of Life Cycle Assessment 8 (6), 324–330.

Khouja, M., 1996. A note on the newsboy problem with an emergency supply option. The Journal of the Operational Research Society 47 (12), 1530–1534.

Khouja, M., 1999. The single-period (news-vendor) problem: Literature review and suggestions for future research. Omega 27 (5), 537–553.

Kim, N., Janic, M., van Wee, B., 2009. Trade-off between carbon dioxide emissions and logistics costs based on multiobjective optimization. Transportation Research Record: Journal of the Transportation Research Board 2139, 107–116.

Klassen, R. D., Johnson, P. F., 2004. The green supply chain. In: New, S., Westbrook, R. (Eds.), Understanding Supply Chains: Concepts, Critique, and Futures. Oxford University Press, pp. 229–251.

Kleindorfer, P. R., Singhal, K., van Wassenhove, L. N., 2005. Sustainable operations management. Production and Operations Managament 14 (4), 482–492.

Klosterhalfen, S., Kiesmüller, G., Minner, S., 2010. A comparison of the constant-order and dual-index policy for dual sourcing. International Journal of Production Economics (In Press, Corrected Proof), –.

Knoll, L., Huth, M., 2008. Emissionshandel aus soziologischer Sicht: Wer handelt eigentlich wie mit Emissionsrechten? UmweltWirtschaftsForum 16 (2), 81–88.

Kruger, J., 2008. Companies and regulators in emission trading programs. In: Antes, R., Bernd, H., Letmathe, P. (Eds.), Emission Trading: Institutional Design, Decision Making and Corporate Strategies. Springer, pp. 3–20.

Lau, A. H.-L., Lau, H.-S., 1988. Maximizing the probability of achieving a target profit in a two-product newsboy problem. Decision Sciences 19 (2), 392–408.

Lau, A. H.-L., Lau, H.-S., 1998. Decision models for single-period products with two ordering opportunities. International Journal of Production Economics 55 (1), 57–70.

Lau, H.-S., 1980. The newsboy problem under alternative optimization objectives. The Journal of the Operational Research Society 31 (6), 525–535.

Letmathe, P., Balakrishnan, N., 2005. Environmental considerations on the optimal product mix. European Journal of Operational Research 167 (2), 398–412.

Li, J., Wang, S., Cheng, T., 2010. Competition and cooperation in a single-retailer two-supplier supply chain with supply disruption. International Journal of Production Economics 124 (1), 137–150.

Linton, J. D., Klassen, R., Jayaraman, V., 2007. Sustainable supply chains: An introduction. Journal of Operations Management 25 (6), 1075–1082.

Mabini, M. C., Pintelon, L. M., Gelders, L. F., 1992. EOQ type formulations for controlling repairable inventories. International Journal of Production Economics 28 (1), 21–33.

Malueg, D. A., Yates, A. J., 2009. Strategic behavior, private information, and decentralization in the European Union Emissions Trading System. Environmental and Resource Economics 43 (3), 413–431.

Minner, S., 2003. Multiple-supplier inventory models in supply chain management: A review. International Journal of Production Economics 81-82 (11), 265–279.

Minner, S., Lindner, G., 2004. Lot-sizing decisions in product recovery management. In: Dekker, R., Fleischmann, M., Inderfurth, K., Van Wassenhove, L. (Eds.), Reverse Logistics – Quantitative Models for Closed-Loop Supply Chains. Springer, pp. 157–179.

Montgomery, W. D., 1972. Markets in licenses and efficient pollution control programs. Journal of Economic Theory 5 (3), 395–418.

Moon, I., Gallego, G., 1994. Distribution free procedures for some inventory models. The Journal of the Operational Research Society 45 (6), 651–658.

Mtalaa, W., Aggoune, R., Schaefers, J., 2009. CO2 emissions calculation models for green supply chain management. In: Proceedings of POMS 20th Annual Meeting.

Nagurney, A., 2000. Sustainable transportation networks. Edward Elgar Publishing Ltd.

Nahmias, S., 2009. Production and Operations Analysis. McGraw-Hill.

Nijkamp, P., van den Bergh, J. C., 1997. New advances in economic modelling and evaluation of environmental issue. European Journal of Operational Research 99 (1), 180–196.

OECD, 2001. Domestic transferable permits for environmental management: Design and implementation. Organisation for Economic Co-Operation and Development.

Pagell, M., Zhaohui, W., 2009. Building a more complete theory of sustainable supply chain management using case studies of 10 exemplars. Journal of Supply Chain Management 45 (2), 37–56.

Pedersen, A. K., 2009. A more sustainable global supply chain. Supply Chain Management Review 13 (7), 6–7.

Penkuhn, T., Spengler, T., Püchert, H., Rentz, O., 1997. Environmental integrated production planning for the ammonia synthesis. European Journal of Operational Research 97 (2), 327–336.

Perrels, A., 2010. User response and equity considerations regarding emission cap-and-trade schemes for travel. Energy Efficiency 3 (2), 149–165.

Piecyk, M., McKinnon, A. C., 2007. Internalising the external costs of road freight transport in the UK. Online.
URL http://www.greenlogistics.org/SiteResources/1fbb59ff-3e5a-4011-a4 1e-18deb8c07fcd_Internalisation%20report%20%28final%29.pdf

Piecyk, M. I., McKinnon, A. C., 2010. Forecasting the carbon footprint of road freight transport in 2020. International Journal of Production Economics 128 (1), 31–42.

Platts, K. W., Song, N., 2010. Overseas sourcing decisions – the total cost of sourcing from China. Supply Chain Management: An International Journal 15 (4), 320–331.

Porter, M. E., Reinhardt, F. L., 2007. A strategic approach to climate. Harvard Business Review 85 (10), 22–26.

Porter, M. E., van der Linde, C., 1995. Green and competitive: Ending the stalemate. Harvard Business Review 73 (5b), 120–134.

Porteus, E. L., 2002. Foundations of Stochastic Inventory Theory. Stanford University Press.

Qin, Y., Wang, R., Vakharia, A. J., Chen, Y., Seref, M. M., 2011. The newsvendor problem: Review and directions for future research. European Journal of Operational Research (In Press, Corrected Proof), –.

Quariguasi Frota Neto, J., Bloemhof-Ruwaard, J., van Nunen, J., van Heck, E., 2008. Designing and evaluating sustainable logistics networks. International Journal of Production Economics 111 (2), 195–208.

Quariguasi Frota Neto, J., Walther, G., Bloemhof, J., van Nunen, J., Spengler, T., 2009a. From closed-loop to sustainable supply chains: The WEEE case. International Journal of Production Research 48 (5), 4463–4481.

Quariguasi Frota Neto, J., Walther, G., Bloemhof, J., van Nunen, J., Spengler, T., 2009b. A methodology for assessing eco-efficiency in logistics networks. European Journal of Operational Research 193 (3), 670–682.

Radulescu, M., Radulescu, S., Radulescu, C. Z., 2009. Sustainable production technologies which take into account environmental constraints. European Journal of Operational Research 193 (3), 730–740.

Ramudhin, A., Chaabane, A., Kharoune, M., Paquet, M., 2008. Carbon market sensitive green supply chain network design. In: Proceedings of the 2008 IEEE IEEM. pp. 1093–1097.

Raux, C., 2004. The use of transferable permits in transport policy. Transportation Research Part D: Transport and Environment 9 (3), 185–197.

Raux, C., 2010. The potential for CO_2 emission trading in transport: The case of personal verhicles and freight. Energy efficiency 3 (2), 133–148.

Rockafellar, R. T., 1997. Convex analysis. Princeton University Press.

Rosič, H., Bauer, G., Jammernegg, W., 2009. A framework for economic and environmental sustainability and resilience of supply chains. In: Reiner, G. (Ed.), Rapid Modelling for Increasing Competitiveness. Springer London, pp. 91–104.

Sankarasubramanian, E., Kumaraswamy, S., 1983. Note on "Optimal ordering quantity to realize a pre-determined level of profit". Management Science 29 (4), 512–514.

Scarf, H. E., 1958. A min-max solution of an inventory problem. In: Arrow, K. J., Karlin, S., Scarf, H. E. (Eds.), Studies in the Mathematical Theory of Inventory and Production. Stanford University Press, pp. 201–209.

Schmidheiny, S., 1992. Changing Course: A Global Business Perspective on Development and the Environment. MIT Press.

Schneider, K., 1998. Comment on M. Hoel, "Emission taxes versus other environmental policies". The Scandinavian Journal of Economics 100 (1), 105–108.

Seuring, S., Müller, M., 2008. From a literature review to a conceptual framework for sustainable supply chain management. Journal of Cleaner Production 16 (15), 1699–1710.

Silver, E. A., Pyke, D. F., Peterson, R., 1998. Inventory Management and Production Planning and Scheduling. Wiley.

Simchi-Levi, D., Kaminsky, P., Simchi-Levi, E., 2008. Designing and managing the supply chain: Concepts, strategies, and case studies. McGraw-Hill.

Sinn, H.-W., 2009. The green paradox. CESifo Forum 10 (3), 10–13.

Smith, A., Watkiss, P., Tweddle, G., McKinnon, A. C., Brown, M., Hunt, A., Treleven, C., Nash, C., Cross, S., 2005. The validity of food miles as an indicator of sustainable development. Online.
URL http://www.defra.gov.uk/evidence/economics/foodfarm/reports/documents/Foodmile.pdf

Sounderpandian, J., Prasad, S., Madan, M., 2008. Supplies from developing countries: Optimal order quantities under loss risks. Omega 36 (1), 122–130.

Srivastava, S. K., 2007. Green supply-chain management: A state-of-the-art literature review. International Journal of Management Reviews 9 (1), 53–80.

Subramanian, R., Talbot, F. B., Gupta, S., 2010. An approach to integrating environmental considerations within managerial decision-making. Journal of Industrial Ecology 14 (3), 378–398.

Suh, S., Huppes, G., 2005. Methods for life cycle inventory of a product. Journal of Cleaner Production 13 (7), 687–697.

Sundarakani, B., de Souza, R., Goh, M., Wagner, S. M., Manikandan, S., 2010. Modeling carbon footprints across the supply chain. International Journal of Production Economics 128 (1), 43–50.

Tang, C. S., 2006. Robust strategies for mitigating supply chain disruptions. International Journal of Logistics: Research and Applications 9 (1), 33–45.

Taplin, D. M. R., Spedding, T. A., Khoo, H. H., 2006. Use of simulation and modelling to develop a sustainable production system. Sustainable Development 14 (3), 149–161.

te Loo, R., 2009. A methodology for calculating CO_2 emissions from transport and an evaluation of the impact of European Union emission regulations. Master's thesis, Technical University Eindhoven.

Teunter, R., 2004. Lot-sizing for inventory systems with product recovery. Computers and Industrial Engineering 46 (3), 431–441.

Teunter, R. H., 2001. Economic ordering quantities for recoverable item inventory systems. Naval Research Logistics 48 (6), 484–495.

The World Bank (Ed.), 2008. International Trade and Climate Change: Economic, Legal, and Institutional Perspectives. The World Bank.

Treitl, S., Rosič, H., Jammernegg, W., 2010. A conceptual framework for the integration of transportation management systems and carbon calculators. In: Reiner, G. (Ed.), Rapid Modelling and Quick Response. Springer, pp. 317–330.

Tsoulfas, G. T., Pappis, C. P., 2006. Environmental principles applicable to supply chains design and operation. Journal of Cleaner Production 14 (18), 1593–1602.

United Nations, 1987. Report of the World Commission on Environment and Development – Our Common Future. United Nations.

van Mieghem, J. A., 2008. Operations Strategy – Principles and Practice. Dynamic Ideas.

Veeraraghavan, S., Scheller-Wolf, A., 2008. Now or later: A simple policy for effective dual sourcing in capacitated systems. Operations Research 56 (4), 850–864.

Venkat, K., 2007. Analyzing and optimizing the environmental performance of supply chains. In: Proceedings of the 2007 ACEEE Summer Study on Energy Efficiency in Industry.

Verfaillie, H. A., Bidwell, R., 2000. Measuring eco-efficiency: A guide to reporting company performance. Online.
URL   http://www.wbcsd.org/web/publications/measuring_eco_efficienc y.pdf

Verhoef, E. T., van den Bergh, J. C. J. M., Button, K. J., 1997. Transport, spatial economy, and the global environment. Environment and Planning A 29 (7), 1195–1213.

Walker, H., Di Sisto, L., McBain, D., 2008. Drivers and barriers to environmental supply chain management practices: Lessons from the public and private sectors. Journal of Purchasing & Supply Management 14 (1), 69–85.

Walter, S., Schmidt, M., 2008. Carbon Footprints und Carbon Label – eine echte Hilfe bei der Kaufentscheidung? UmweltWirtschaftsForum 16 (3), 175–181.

Warburton, R. D., Stratton, R., 2002. Questioning the relentless shift to offshore manufacturing. Supply Chain Management: An International Journal 7 (2), 101–108.

Warburton, R. D., Stratton, R., 2005. The optimal quantity of quick response manufacturing for an onshore and offshore sourcing model. International Journal of Logistics: Research and Applications 8 (2), 125–141.

Wiedmann, T., Minx, J., 2008. A definition of 'carbon footprint'. In: Pertsova, C. C. (Ed.), Ecological Economics Research Trends. Nova Science Publishers, pp. 1–11.

Wirl, F., 1991. Evaluation of management strategies under environmental constraints. European Journal of Operational Research 55 (2), 191–200.

Wirl, F., 1995. Auswirkungen von Umweltsteuern auf die optimalen Produktionsstrategien in einem Modell der Produktion und Lagerhaltung. Zeitschrift für betriebswirtschaftliche Forschung 47 (5), 456–465.

World Business Council on Sustainable Developement, 2000. Eco-efficiency: Creating more value with less impact. Online.
URL http://www.wbcsd.org/web/publications/eco_efficiency_creating_m ore_value.pdf

Wu, H.-J., Dunn, S. C., 1995. Environmentally responsible logisitcs systems. International Journal of Physical Distribution & Logistics Management 25 (2), 20–38.

Xepapadeas, A. P., 1992. Environmental policy, adjustment costs, and behavior of the firm. Journal of Environmental Economics and Management 23 (3), 258–275.

Yazlali, Ö., Erhun, F., 2008. Managing demand uncertainty with dual supply contracts on capacity and inventory: A heuristic approach. Working Paper, Stanford University.

Yu, H., Zeng, A. Z., Zhao, L., 2009. Single or dual sourcing: Decision-making in the presence of supply chain disruption risks. Omega 37 (4), 788–800.

Zavanella, L., Zanoni, S., 2009. Energy and inventories. In: Jaber, M. Y. (Ed.), Inventory Management: Non-Classical Views. Taylor & Francis Ltd., pp. 75–98.

Zhang, B., Du, S., 2010. Multi-product newsboy problem with limited capacity and outsourcing. European Journal of Operational Research 202 (1), 107–113.

Zhou, S. X., Chao, X., 2010. Newsvendor bounds and heuristics for serial supply chains with regular and expedited shipping. Naval Research Logistics 57 (1), 71–87.

Forschungsergebnisse der Wirtschaftsuniversität Wien

Herausgeber: Wirtschaftsuniversität Wien –
vertreten durch a.o. Univ. Prof. Dr. Barbara Sporn

INFORMATION UND KONTAKT:

WU (Wirtschaftsuniversität Wien)
Department of Finance, Accounting and Statistics
Institute for Finance, Banking and Insurance
Heiligenstädter Straße 46-48, 1190 Wien
Tel.: 0043-1-313 36/4556
Fax: 0043-1-313 36/904556
valentine.wendling@wu.ac.at
www.wu.ac.at/finance

Band 39   Astrid Haider: Die Lohnhöhe und Lohnstreuung im Nonprofit-Sektor. Eine quantitative Analyse anhand österreichischer Arbeitnehmer-Arbeitgeber-Daten. 2010.

Band 40   Maureen Lenhart: Pflegekräftemigration nach Österreich. Eine empirische Analyse. 2010.

Band 41   Oliver Schwank: Linkages in South African Economic Development. Industrialisation without Diversification? 2010.

Band 42   Judith Kast-Aigner: A Corpus-Based Analysis of the Terminology of the European Union's Development Cooperation Policy, with the African, Caribbean and Pacific Group of States. 2010.

Band 43   Emel Arikan: Single Period Inventory Control and Pricing. An Empirical and Analytical Study of a Generalized Model. 2011.

Band 44   Gerhard Wohlgenannt: Learning Ontology Relations by Combining Corpus-Based Techniques and Reasoning on Data from Semantic Web Sources. 2011.

Band 45   Thomas Peschta: Der Einfluss von Kundenzufriedenheit auf die Kundenloyalität und die Wirkung der Wettbewerbsintensität am Beispiel der Gemeinschaftsverpflegungsgastronomie. 2011.

Band 46   Friederike Hehle: Die Anwendung des Convenience-Konzepts auf den Betriebstyp Vending. 2011.

Band 47   Thomas Herzog: Strategisches Management von Koopetition. Eine empirisch begründete Theorie im industriellen Kontext der zivilen Luftfahrt. 2011.

Band 48   Christian Weismayer: Statische und longitudinale Zufriedenheitsmessung. 2011.

Band 49   Johannes Fichtinger: The Single-Period Inventory Model with Spectral Risk Measures. 2011.

Band 50   Isabella R. Hatak: Kompetenz, Vertrauen und Kooperation. Eine experimentelle Studie. 2011.

Band 51   Birgit Gusenbauer: Der Beitrag der Prospect Theory zur Beschreibung und Erklärung von Servicequalitätsurteilen und Kundenzufriedenheit im Kontext von Versicherungsentscheidungen. 2012.

Band 52   Markus A. Höllerer: Between Creed, Rhetoric Façade, and Disregard. Dissemination and Theorization of Corporate Social Responsibility in Austria. 2012.

Band 53   Jakob Müllner: Die Wirkung von Private Equity auf das Wachstum und die Internationalisierung. Eine empirische Impact-Studie des österreichischen Private Equity Marktes. 2012.

Band 54   Heidrun Rosič: The Economic and Environmental Sustainability of Dual Sourcing. 2012.

www.peterlang.de